Welcome to Charleston

1

Charleston, South Carolina
© Ch. Heeb/hemis.fr

Getting to Charleston

BY PLANE

From Charleston International Airport (CHS)

5500 International Blvd. - ☎843-767-7000 - www.chs-airport.com. Charleston has one major airport, located 12 miles west of downtown, off I-526.

A **taxi** from the airport to downtown costs approximately $30. Ride-sharing options like Lyft and Uber will cost a bit less, starting from $17.

Shuttle service – A more economical alternative to a taxi, shuttles are available right after you leave baggage claim area. Shuttle service to downtown is $14 per person, payable by cash or card.

BY BUS

The **Charleston Regional Transportation Authority** (CARTA; www.ridecarta.com) offers bus service to and from the airport via the **North Area Shuttle** (NASH) Express ($3.50). The CARTA stop is just outside of baggage claim. Shuttles run daily on the hour, 8am-midnight, and stop at the North Charleston Visitor Center (975-B Centre Point Dr.) and Tanger Outlet en route to the downtown stop at the Charleston Visitor Center (375 Meeting St.). The trip takes 30 min.

The NASH shuttle (Express 4 Route) makes no stops when running from downtown to the airport.

The Route 11 CARTA bus route also operates from the airport. ($2; exact fare change required). The bus departs every 30 min. from the stop located near the passenger pick-up area. Travel to downtown takes 60 min. The downtown stop is at Meeting and Mary Sts., next to the Charleston Visitor Center.

BY CAR

Downtown Charleston is an easy 30-min. drive from the airport, via I-526 to I-26East, which leads directly to the city. Rental cars (from Avis, Hertz, National, Enterprise and Budget) are available at the airport.

3

Dock Street Theatre, Charleston
© J. Arnold Images/hemis.fr

Unmissable

Our picks for must-see sites:

Charleston Historic District ★★★ p. 14

Drayton Hall★★★ p. 42

Nathaniel Russell House★★★ p. 14

Fort Sumter National Monument ★★★ p. 52

Middleton Place and Gardens★★★ p. 46

The Battery ★★
♿ p. 19

**South Carolina
Aquarium ★★** ♿ p. 26

**Patriots Point Naval &
Maritime Museum ★★**
♿ p. 56

5

Magnolia Plantation ★★
♿ p. 49

**Circular Congregational
Church ★★**
♿ p. 40

Our favorites

❤ **A walk along The Battery** reveals an eyeful of quintessential Charleston. Views of the Cooper River and pastel-colored columned mansions—some of the most beautiful residential architecture in the city—abound along this oleander-lined promenade.

❤ **A horse-drawn carriage tour** may be touristy, but it's a great way for first-time visitors to get an orientation to the city and its history at a clip-clop pace. You'll find the carriages of several tour companies lined up and ready to go along Market Street at Anson Street.

❤ **Shop at the Old City Market** for made-in-Charleston souvenirs. As you peruse the wares in the vendor stalls, be sure to stop and chat with the artisans making coiled sweetgrass baskets. These women are preserving a dying art that West African slaves brought to South Carolina more than 300 years ago.

❤ **Watch the sunset from a rooftop bar** while you sip a cocktail, and you'll have a 360-degree view of the city. Charleston boasts numerous rooftop watering holes, where all of the peninsula and the surrounding harbor stretches out in the distance.

❤ **Relax aboard the Schooner Pride,** and see the city from a different angle. Modeled after the 19C trading schooners that once plied Charleston Harbor, this three-masted ship provides a two-hour respite from the Historic District crowds, as you enjoy the cool breezes and drink in the serenity of the sea.

❤ **Get inspired at Middleton Place Gardens.** Laid out in the grand classical style of 18C European gardens, America's oldest landscaped garden stretches down grassy lawns to the Ashley River. No matter what time of year you go, there's always something blooming—from camellias in January to magnolias in June.

❤ **Take a shrimp and grits lunch break.** You can't leave Charleston without trying this signature Lowcountry dish. There are as many different versions as there are restaurants that serve it, so refer to the restaurant listing to find your favorite. .

❤ **Visit the Charleston Farmer's Market** on Saturday morning (Apr-Nov) in Marion Square. Have breakfast there—anything from fresh-baked pastries to barbecue—then check out the more than 100 vendors who sell locally harvested salt, stone-ground grits, handmade pasta, South Carolina shrimp, and produce from area farms.

Ghost and Dungeon Walking Tour

💜 **Experience Charleston's haunted history on a Ghost Tour.** Leave the little ones at home as you walk through some of the city's most haunted sites and graveyards after dark and listen to the spooky tales of the spirits who still roam the Historic District.

💜 **See a show at Dock Street Theatre.** It's not often you can see a contemporary show (think *Avenue Q* and *Shakespeare in Love*) in America's oldest theater. With its graceful wrought-iron exterior balcony and its wood-lined performing space, Dock Street Theatre is home to the Charleston Stage Company.

💜 **Hunt for Antiques on King Street.** If you're looking for treasures form the past, haunt the blocks of King Street between Market and Broad streets for purveyors of 18C and 19C English furniture, Louis XV bergère chairs, crystal chandeliers, and fine silver and china.

💜 **Spend a day at the beach.** It's a short drive across the Ashley River to nearby Folly Beach, where you can soak up some sun and fish from the pier.

Charleston in 3 days

DAY 1

▶ *Morning*

The best way to get your bearings in Charleston is to take a tour of the **Historic District★★★**. Depending on your preference, you can choose a guided walking tour or a horse-drawn carriage tour. If you'd rather explore on your own, be sure to walk along **The Battery★★** for river views and a look at some of the city's gorgeous 18C and 19C homes.

▶ *Midday*

On your way along The Battery (East Bay Street), stop and pick up some picnic fare to take to **White Point Gardens★** at the tip of the peninsula.

▶ *Afternoon*

If you can tear yourself away from the waterfront, walk back along Meeting Street and tour the **Nathaniel Russell House★★★** and **Calhoun Mansion★★** to see how Charleston's elite lived in the 19C. Farther west on Meeting Street, be sure to stop by the distinctive Romanesque Revival **Circular Congregational Church★★**.

▶ *Evening*

Before a leisurely dinner (make reservations well in advance) at one of the Holy City's divine restaurants, stop to savor the sunset from one of the Historic District's **rooftop bars**.

©Gwen Cannon/Michelin

Japanese Gardens, Calhoun Mansion

If you have one more day . . .

*There's so much more to see and do: Drive over the Ravenel Bridge to **Patriots Point Naval and Maritime Museum**★★ in Mt. Pleasant and explore the decks of the WWII aircraft carrier, the USS Yorktown. Back on the peninsula, journey farther back in time and tour the **Edmondston-Alston House**★★ (and the **Heyward-Washington House**★★ which boasts a lovely collection of 18C Charleston-made furniture.*

DAY 2

▶ Morning
Hop a cruise to **Fort Sumter National Monument**★★★ to see where the first shots of the Civil War were fired. The cruise and the fort tour will take all morning.

▶ Midday
Head to nearby East Bay Street for a casual lunch of local seafood in one of our recommended **restaurants.**

▶ Afternoon
After lunch, check out the marine life exhibits at the **South Carolina Aquarium**★★, which is adjacent to the boat dock where the ferries to Fort Sumter operate. From there, it's only a few blocks to the **Charleston Museum**★ and its exquisite collection of 18C and 19C Charleston silver.

▶ Evening
After dinner in one of the stellar restaurants on **upper King Street** stay to experience one or two of the cool clubs and bars in that area. If you're on foot and don't feel like walking, you can always take a **pedicab** or a **Charleston Rickshaw** (👆p. 172) back to your hotel.

DAY 3

▶ Morning
Take a short ride to Ashley River Road to tour **Drayton Hall**★★★, one of the best examples of Georgian-Palladian architecture in America. While you're in the area, drive down the road to **Middleton Place**★★★, another former plantation, known for its gorgeous **gardens**★★★.

▶ Midday
Visit the newly renovated **Gibbes Museum of Art**★, for a look at its collection of fine art from the American South. For lunch, you need not go any farther than the museum's new cafe, The Daily by Butcher & Bee.

▶ Afternoon
Afterwards, stroll through the **Old City Market**★★ to shop for locally made souvenirs—and don't miss the artisan-made sweetgrass baskets.

▶ Evening
Catch a performance—perhaps a concert by the Charleston Symphony—at the new **Gaillard Center**, then make your way to the **Bar at Husk**, celebrity chef Sean Brock's bar (next to his acclaimed restaurant of the same name), which touts an amazing bourbon list, as well as creative craft cocktails in a restored late-19C house.

9

Discovering Charleston

Rainbow Row, Charleston
© H. Looney/DanitaDelimont.com/age fotostock

Charleston today

Steeped in history and hailed for its Southern hospitality, Charleston, South Carolina, never fails to disappoint. After all, there's a reason—many, actually—that the city is consistently lauded as one of the top destinations in the United States. Anchoring the coast on a narrow peninsula of land where the Ashley and Cooper rivers converge, South Carolina's oldest city dazzles visitors with the cobblestone streets, delightful gardens and colonial homes (some of which are open for tours) that populate the 5.2-square-mile **Historic District**. It is here that visitors flock to tour historic homes and museums, ogle the stunning architecture, delve into local history, troll the shops on King Street, and

eat and drink their way through the city's plethora of stellar restaurants and bars.

The city of Charleston may be small (population 128,000), but for its size, it boasts a wealth of attractions. You'll find the majority of them within the Historic District, concentrated east of Calhoun Street, which bisects the peninsula. The peninsula narrows to a point where the two rivers meet, its two edges defined by East Bay Street and Murray Boulevard. West of Calhoun, King Street is known as **Upper King**, revitalized blocks that now hold tony shops and many of the city's best bars and restaurants. Just outside the Historic District, the neighborhood known as **NoMo** (for North Morrison, the continuation of

Charleston Firsts

- America's first theater, the **Dock Street Theater**★ (◉ see p. 31), opened in 1736 in a building (later destroyed by fire) on the corner of Church and Dock Street (now Queen St.)
- The first fire insurance agency, the Friendly Society for the Mutual Insuring of Houses Against Fire was founded in 1736. It went bankrupt four years later, after the fire of 1740 destroyed more than 300 buildings.
- The College of Charleston, which opened its doors in 1770, was America's first municipal college.
- Founded in 1773, **The Charleston Museum**★ (◉ see p. 31) claims bragging rights to being the country's first museum.
- America's first Chamber of Commerce was organized in Charleston in 1773.
- The first shots of the Civil War were fired in Charleston Harbor at **Fort Sumter**★★★ (◉ see p. 52) on April 12, 1861.

East Bay Street) is blossoming with new restaurants and breweries. Just to whet your appetite, the **Gibbes Museum of Art** recently reopened following a major renovation, and now displays more of its impressive collection of art from the American South. Kids will love clip-clopping through the Historic District on a horse-drawn carriage ride and meeting local marine denizens up-close at the **South Carolina Aquarium**. And who can resist the district's fine art and antique galleries, and the local wares in the stalls that line the **Old City Market**?

Off the Peninsula

Beyond the peninsula's borders lie white-sand beaches, resort islands and historic sites. Visit the original site of the colonial city at **Charles Towne Landing**, and take a cruise to **Fort Sumter**, which saw the first shots of the Civil War. A short drive to Ashley River Road on Charleston's west side reveals **antebellum plantations** and gardens that will easily require two days to visit. Just across the Cooper River in Mt. Pleasant is **Patriots Point Naval and Maritime Museum**.

Lowcountry Coast

To the north of Charleston, **Myrtle Beach** is tops for family fun, with its wide beaches, golf courses and entertainment venues galore. A little over an hour's drive south, you'll come to the picturesque riverfront hamlet of **Beaufort**, which ranks as South Carolina's second-oldest city.

Hilton Head Island, 30 miles south of Beaufort, appeals for the myriad hotels, condominiums, golf courses and tennis facilities.

Planned residential communities now cover land once occupied by cotton plantations.

Just over 100 miles south of Charleston, you'll come to **Savannah**, a city that stands out for the grid of grassy squares that mark the downtown historic district. **Georgia's Golden Isles** await farther south still. This string of Atlantic barrier islands lures visitors with gleaming sands and the 19C «summer cottages» of America's former millionaires.

A destination for all seasons

With its subtropical climate, the South Carolina Coast is a great place to visit year-round. The best times to come, weather-wise—spring and fall—are also the most crowded. Summers in the Lowcountry are hot and humid—sometimes oppressively so—but that doesn't stop sun-seekers from packing the beaches up and down the coast. In fall, the beach crowds go home, and golfers turn out to enjoy the crisp, clear weather on area courses. It's not uncommon to have 60°F (16°C) days in January, when hotel rates are considerably lower. Like any gracious Southerner, Charleston welcomes visitors no matter the time of year. Any season is a good one to bask on the area's wide sandy beaches, revel in its historic architecture, and breathe its magnolia-scented air.

Historic District★★★

Any visit to Charleston should begin on the lower tip of the 5.2-square-mile peninsula formed by the Ashley and Cooper rivers. This area composes the Historic District★★★, the heart of Charleston since 1680. It encompasses the land specified in the original 17C Grand Modell, or city plan. As you stroll the palmetto-studded streets lined with gas lanterns, it's easy to imagine the colonial days when Charleston was London in miniature—a prosperous aristocratic city whose gentry built many of the splendid houses you see today. Here, you'll discover some of the city's legendary sights and its loveliest structures, along with a multitude of boutiques, antiques shops and restaurants that cater to a wide range of tastes and pocketbooks.

▶**Tip:** Consider purchasing an attractions pass that offers discounted admission to a number of historic sites. See www.charlestoncvb.com.

14

NATHANIEL RUSSELL HOUSE★★★

51 Meeting St. - ℘843-723-1623 - www.historiccharleston.org - Visit by 30-minute guided tour only, year-round daily 10am–5pm - Closed Thanksgiving, Dec 24–25 - $12 - Combination tickets ($18) are available for Nathaniel Russell and Aiken-Rhett houses, both of which are operated by the Historic Charleston Foundation. ♿

If you just see one historic house in Charleston, make it this one. The sister property to the Aiken-Rhett House, the 3-story, 9-room Nathaniel Russell House has been restored to its 19C glory after the roof collapsed when Hurricane Hugo blew through town in 1989. The brick residence, considered to be one of the best examples of Federal-style architecture in the US, was built in 1808 for Nathaniel Russell and his wife, Sarah. Born in Rhode Island, Russell came to Charleston at age 27 in 1765, as an agent for a Providence import-export firm. When he moved his family into the new house in 1808, Russell was 70 years old, and ranked as one of the city's wealthiest merchants.

You can see his prosperity for yourself in the ornate carved woodwork and moldings, and the collections of fine 18C Charleston-made antiques and English silver that decorate the lovely rooms.

Interior

The Nathaniel Russell House is famed for its **flying staircase★★★**, a freestanding spiral that circles up, seemingly unsupported, to the third floor. Rooms are laid out in identical symmetrical suites (rectangular, oval, square) on each of the three floors.

Nathaniel Russell House

Garden, Nathaniel Russell House

©Historic Charleston Foundation

16

The oval **Music Room** was used routinely for entertaining Charleston's elite. Resembling windows, the room's large paneled mirrors were intended to reflect the firelight.

Gardens

A formal English garden flanks the house with boxwood hedges and plants favored by 19C Charlestonians. An amateur gardener, Mrs. Russell first festooned this «urban plantation»

Hey, Honey, Wanna Joggle?

The first thing the tour guide will point out to you at Nathaniel Russell House is the ***joggling board****, which looks like a sort of garden seat. You might think it's a children's toy—and indeed, kids throughout the centuries have loved them—but in 19C Charleston, joggling boards were used more often by courting couples. It's said that a home that had a joggling board never had an unmarried daughter. Try it with a friend and see for yourself: as you bounce gently on the board, your partner will slip closer and closer. To get one for your garden, contact the* ***Old Charleston Joggling Board Company*** *(1601 Oceanic St. - ℘843-414-4080 - www.jogglingboard.com).*

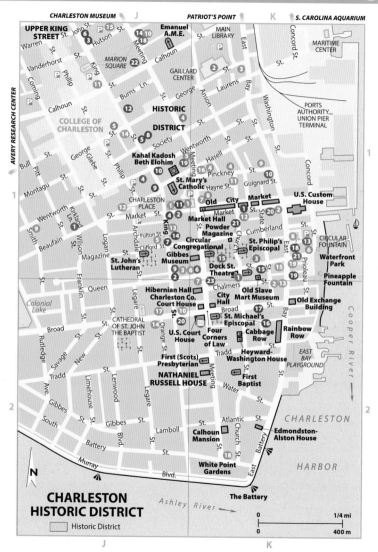

CHARLESTON MUSEUM J PATRIOT'S POINT K S. CAROLINA AQUARIUM

UPPER KING STREET

Emanuel A.M.E.

MAIN LIBRARY

MARITIME CENTER

MARION SQUARE

GAILLARD CENTER

PORTS AUTHORITY UNION PIER TERMINAL

HISTORIC

COLLEGE OF CHARLESTON

DISTRICT

Kahal Kadosh Beth Elohim

St. Mary's Catholic

U.S. Custom House

CHARLESTON PLACE

Old City Market

Market Hall

Powder Magazine

CIRCULAR FOUNTAIN

St. Philip's Episcopal

Waterfront Park

Circular Congregational

Gibbes Museum

St. John's Lutheran

Pineapple Fountain

Dock St. Theatre

Hibernian Hall

Charleston Co. Court House

City Hall

Old Slave Mart Museum

Old Exchange Building

Colonial Lake

CATHEDRAL OF ST. JOHN THE BAPTIST

U.S. Court House

Four Corners of Law

St. Michael's Episcopal

Cabbage Row

Rainbow Row

Heyward-Washington House

EAST BAY PLAYGROUND

First (Scots) Presbyterian

NATHANIEL RUSSELL HOUSE

First Baptist

CHARLESTON

Calhoun Mansion

Edmondston-Alston House

White Point Gardens

HARBOR

The Battery

N

CHARLESTON HISTORIC DISTRICT

Historic District

Ashley River

0   1/4 mi
0   400 m

J   K

17

Aiken-Rhett House

©Historic Charleston Foundation

with flowers, myrtle bowers, and lemon and orange trees.

AIKEN-RHETT HOUSE★★

48 Elizabeth St. - ☎843-723-1159 - www.historiccharleston.org - Visit by 30-minute guided tour only, year-round daily 10am-5pm - Closed Thanksgiving, Dec 24-25 - $12 - Combination tickets ($18) available for Nathaniel Russell and Aiken-Rhett houses.

The difference between conservation and restoration will be clear after you visit the Aiken-Rhett House and the Nathaniel Russell House, its sister property, both of which are maintained by the Historic Charleston Foundation. Unlike other Charleston historic houses that have been restored to their former elegance, the 12-room Aiken-Rhett House has been preserved as it appeared c.1860, just before the Civil War.

Built as a Federal-style brick double house (☜see p. 14) in 1817, the house was purchased in 1827 by wealthy cotton merchant William Aiken Sr. After his death, his only son, William Jr., inherited the house with his wife, Harriet. The new owners made significant changes to the structure, moving the front entrance, building a large addition, and reconfiguring the first floor with an arched marble entry-hall staircase, gracious double parlors and an art gallery. The couple

Single House

As you wander through the Historic District, you'll notice narrow houses where the porch faces the side instead of the street. This type of dwelling is known as a Single House, Charleston's distinctive contribution to American architecture, which is based on a typical West Indian design (many of Charleston's early settlers were planters from Barbados). The typical single house is one room wide and at least two rooms deep, and includes a long piazza—the Charlestonian term for the airy porches designed to catch prevailing breezes—lying behind a false front door on the narrow side of the house. The real entrance to the house is off the piazza. A variation on this theme, the Double House is a nearly square structure with a room in each corner, divided by a central hall.

returned from travels in Europe with fine paintings and sumptuous furnishings, some of which can still be seen in the house.

Aiken, who served as governor of South Carolina from 1844 to 1846, was a well-to-do rice planter. After his death in 1887, Harriet converted the ballroom into her bedroom and closed off several rooms, furnishings and all. After Harriet's death, her daughter did little to maintain the house, except to add electricity to several of the rooms. When the Historic Charleston Foundation acquired the crumbling property in 1995, they opted to clean, stabilize and preserve it, just as they'd found it.

Interior

Today, the eerie ravages of time are evident in the rooms, especially in the occasional pieces of original furniture with their tattered fabric, and in the peeling wallpaper—but that's all part of the property's charm.

Grounds

Out back, the original 1817 outbuildings (typical of every 19C town house in Charleston) include the slaves' quarters, kitchen and stable.

THE BATTERY ★★

16 Meeting St.

If you've seen any photographs at all of Charleston, chances are you've seen the Battery—it figures prominently on almost every advertisement for the city (and on every other souvenir you'll find in town). Indeed, this Historic District landmark defines the tip of Charleston's peninsula.

Long considered a strategic point from which to defend the city, The Battery takes its nickname from its military service. The site is protected by a high seawall that lines the Cooper River side of Charleston Harbor. This wall replaced the masonry structure built in 1700 to fortify the city. Strengthened over the years to ward off hurricanes—including Hurricane Hugo in 1989—the wall became known as the High Battery for the gun emplacement stationed here during the War of 1812.

19

21 East Battery Bed & Breakfast

21 East Battery - ✆843-722-6606 or ✆800-743-3583 - www.21eastbattery. com - Rates start at $265. You may not be able to spend the night in the Edmondston-Alston House, but you can stay on the grounds of this urban complex in Charles Edmondston's 1825 carriage house. Now a B&B, the inn offers guests a choice of a one-bedroom carriage house and a separate two-story house with two bedrooms and two baths. Rates include breakfast and a complimentary tour of the Edmondston-Alston House.

20

Earthen batteries were constructed during the Civil War, although they never saw much action. After the war ended in 1865, the Battery reverted to more peaceful uses as a park, now graced with statues, fountains, trees and plantings.

Views★★★

Walkers, joggers and hosts of visitors frequent the pretty oleander-lined promenade to savor views of the Cooper River to the east and Charleston Harbor to the south. The graceful mansions that line the East and South Battery (depending on which side of the corner they're located) are dowagers that have withstood many a storm. Views stretch out over the water to distant Fort Sumter and Sullivans Island.

Architecture★★★

The elegant pastel-painted mansions set along the Battery, positioned so that their airy piazzas catch the prevailing breezes off the river, provide stellar examples of Charleston's noted antebellum residential architecture.

CALHOUN MANSION★★

16 Meeting St. - ✆843-722-8205 - www.calhounmansion.net - Visit by 30-minute guided tour only, Mar-Nov daily 11am-5pm (last tour 5pm); Rest of the year daily 11am-4:30pm - Closed Thanksgiving, Dec 25 - $17.
With 24,000 square feet of living space, the 3-story Calhoun Mansion ranks as Charleston's largest single residence. Built in 1876 in the Italianate style for banker George Williams, the home was designed by Virginia architect W. P. Russell. Upon Williams' death in 1903, the house passed to his daughter Sarah and her husband, Patrick Calhoun (grandson of statesman John C. Calhoun). In 1910 it was remodeled by Louis Comfort Tiffany. Now a private residence, the home is filled with the owner's furnishings, paintings and sculptures collected around the world. The mansion encompasses 35 rooms, many of which retain the exquisite original satinwood, black walnut and chestnut woodwork, Minton tiles and ornate gasoliers.
For a tour of the entire mansion, including the Italianate tower, sign up for the hour-long **Grand Tour** (*$75 - reservations required*).

© Gwen Cannon/Michelin

Calhoun Mansion

Interior

The **Main Hallway** holds the sole piece of furniture belonging to George Williams: the 24-seat dining table (displayed without its leaves). In the **Reception Room**, richly appointed widow cornices are original to the house. The airy second-floor **Music Room** rises 35 feet to a large glass skylight, crafted by Louis Tiffany, in the covered ceiling.

Charleston Renaissance

Charleston's renaissance was a cultural one. In the mid-1920s, Charleston's antebellum mansions were crumbling, its economy depressed. Enter a group of local artists and writers who sought to bring attention to the city's rich cultural heritage. Writer DuBose Heyward—who penned the 1925 book Porgy, on which composer George Gershwin based his folk opera Porgy and Bess in 1935—and Charleston painter Elizabeth O'Neill Verner, along with others, all interpreted the Lowcountry folkways in their art. Their music, books and canvases created images of daily life of Charleston and the nearby plantations for the world to see. The cultural renewal they launched, later known as the Charleston Renaissance, emphasized American values and realism. The sense of civic pride it fostered eventually sparked Charleston's historic-preservation movement.

Thomas Elfe

Born in England, Thomas Elfe emigrated o Charles Towne in 1747 and established himself as a tradesman in the thriving city. His skill soon made him one of the most sought-after cabinetmakers in the area, and a wealthy man in his day. Inspired by his contemporary Thomas Chippendale, Elfe made more than 1,500 pieces between 1768 and his death in 1775, including beds, chairs, bookcases and desks. In the mid-18C, Thomas Elfe lived in the house at 54 Queen Street. Today you can see examples of Elfe's fine work at the Heyward-Washington House and at The Charleston Museum.

22 Gardens

Highlight of the gardens is the **Southern Garden** with its boxwood ring encircling 15 rounded hedges and its centerpiece 19C statue of Mercury. The **Eastern Garden** features a central fountain symmetrically flanked by koi ponds underlaid with intricate brickwork. At the rear of the house, the elaborate **Japanese Gardens** are adorned with a large fountain and a columned archway wrapped with Japanese wisteria. The ornate iron gate and fencing incorporating a rope pattern are original to the property.

EDMONDSTON-ALSTON HOUSE★★

21 East Battery - ℘843-722-7171 - http://www.edmondstonalston.com/ - Visit by 30-minute guided tour only Tue-Sat 10am-4:30pm; Sun and Mon 1pm-4:30pm - Closed Thanksgiving, Dec 25 - $12.

Imagine what tales this stunning house could tell, overlooking the harbor as it has since 1825, when it was built for Scotsman and cotton trader Charles Edmondston as the first house on the High Battery. When the cotton market turned sour 13 years later, Edmondston sold the property to Charleston rice planter Colonel William Alston, whose son, Charles, added the third-floor piazza and other Greek Revival details. A tour of the exquisitely decorated mansion, with its three airy piazzas supported by Doric and Corinthian columns, depicts the life of Charleston's 19C elite. Here you'll find Alston family furnishings, silver, and a collection of more than 1,000 rare volumes in Charles Alston's second-floor library.

HEYWARD-WASHINGTON HOUSE★★

187 Church St. - ℘843-722-2996 - www.charlestonmuseum.org - Visit by 30-minute guided tour only, year-round Mon-Sat, 10am-5pm; Sun noon -5pm - Closed major holidays - $12 - Combination tickets available for Heyward-Washington House, Joseph Manigault House, and The Charleston Museum.

Named for Thomas Heyward, its original double house, this redbrick double house remains structurally unchanged from 1772 when it was built within the boundaries of the old walled city. George Washington slept here during a visit to Charleston in 1791—thus the second part of the home's name.

Edmondston-Alston House

© The Charleston Museum

Heyward-Washington House

Heyward distinguished himself as a signer of the Declaration of Independence, as a criminal court judge and as an officer in the South Carolina militia during the Revolution. A tour of his home gives a first-hand glimpse at the luxuries a man of his status enjoyed in colonial Charleston. Outside, you can see the original kitchen, and a formal garden containing symmetrical plots of camellias, tea olives, boxwood, roses and herbs—all plants introduced to the Lowcountry before 1791.

Furniture Collection★
Inside, the rooms are decorated with a fine collection of 18C Charleston-made furniture, including the priceless Holmes bookcase—which survived British mortar fire during the Revolutionary War—as well as pieces attributed to colonial cabinetmaker Thomas Elfe.

OLD CITY MARKET★★

On Market St. between Meeting and E. Bay Sts. - ♿.
A trip to Charleston just isn't complete without a stroll through the Old City Market. Stretching from Meeting Street to the river along Market Street, the three-block-long row of open-air sheds with arched openings fills daily with vendors selling everything from sweetgrass

24

Heyward-Washington House

Market Hall

26

Market Hall★

Market St. at Meeting St.
You'll know you're at the market when you see the stately 1841 Greek Revival landmark presiding over the market sheds. Designed by architect Edward Brickell White, Market Hall resembles a Roman temple. The structure was restored to its 19C grandeur—to the tune of $3.6 million—after sustaining severe damage during Hurricane Hugo in 1989. Although Market Hall's exterior may look like stone, it's really made from brick covered with stucco scored to resemble stone blocks. The brownstone steps and trim take on a reddish hue in the sunlight. A recent renovation enclosed and air-conditioned the Great Hall. Sheep and bull skulls on the stucco frieze refer to the 19C meat market that once stood here. Market Hall now houses a substantial collection of Civil War memorabilia on its second floor.

SOUTH CAROLINA AQUARIUM★★

100 Aquarium Wharf, at the east end of Calhoun St. - ✆843-577-3474 - www.scaquarium.org - Open year-round daily 9am-5pm - Closed Thanksgiving, half-day Dec 24 (open 9am-noon), Dec 25 - $29.95 adults; $22.95 children (ages 3–12) - Free for children under age 3 - Café - ♿.

baskets to T-shirts. The site where the stalls now stand used to be marshland belonging to the Pinckney family, wealthy planters who donated it for use as a city market in the late 1700s. At the turn of the 19C, the swampy plot was filled in to create a meat and produce market. For years, the market served as the commercial hub of the city.

Charleston City Night Market

Showcasing more than 100 local artists and craftspeople, the Night Market takes place at the Old City Market on Friday and Saturday evenings (6:30-10:30pm) from April through December. Come out and shop for locally made goods from candles to clothing and enjoy live entertainment at this festive evening event.

Rows of Row Houses

An iconic image of Charleston, the multicolored row of colonial town houses known as **Rainbow Row** *(79-107 E. Bay St.) reigns as the largest intact cluster of Georgian row houses in the US. The earliest of these dwellings, built as merchants' residences, dates back to 1740.*

In the 1920s, poor residents of the late-18C double tenement called **Cabbage Row** *(89-91 Church St.) sold vegetables from their windowsills. These homes provided the inspiration for "Catfish Row" in Charleston native Dubose Heyward's 1925 novel Porgy. Heyward's story became the basis for George Gershwin's folk opera Porgy and Bess, a fictional look at African-American life in 1920s Charleston. Today the dwellings house shops.*

© PhotoDisc

Rainbow Row

If you've ever wondered what kinds of creatures inhabit the waters around Charleston, you'll learn the answer here. From seahorses to sharks, more than 6,000 creatures and 12,000 plants fill the aquarium's nine galleries. Opened in 2000, the contemporary two-level facility overlooks Charleston Harbor and the Cooper River.

Exhibits focus on seven watery environments found in South Carolina,

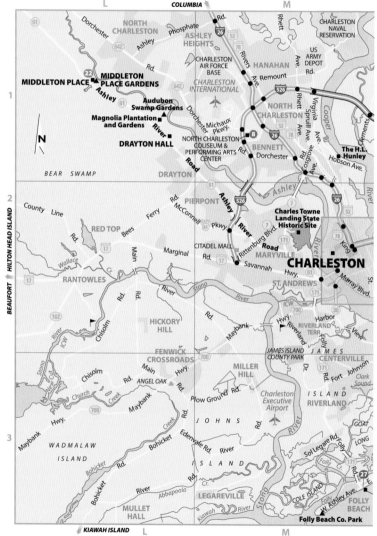

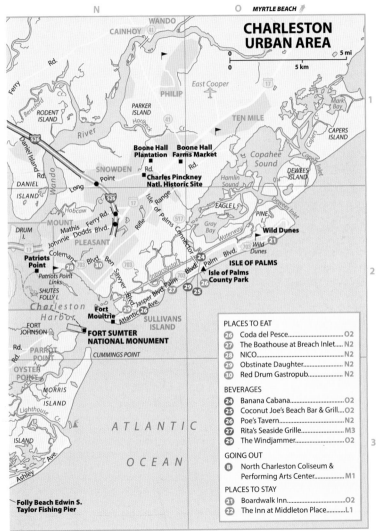

CHARLESTON URBAN AREA

0 — 5 mi
0 — 5 km

MYRTLE BEACH

PLACES TO EAT
26	Coda del Pesce	O2
27	The Boathouse at Breach Inlet	N2
28	NICO	N2
29	Obstinate Daughter	N2
30	Red Drum Gastropub	N2

BEVERAGES
24	Banana Cabana	O2
25	Coconut Joe's Beach Bar & Grill	O2
26	Poe's Tavern	N2
27	Rita's Seaside Grille	M3
29	The Windjammer	O2

GOING OUT
| 8 | North Charleston Coliseum & Performing Arts Center | M1 |

PLACES TO STAY
| 21 | Boardwalk Inn | O2 |
| 22 | The Inn at Middleton Place | L1 |

29

Fast Facts About Sea Turtles

- *The Loggerhead sea turtle is the state reptile of South Carolina.*
- *Loggerheads can live up to 50 years or more.*
- *The largest sea turtle in the world is the leatherback, which can weigh up to 2,000 lbs.*
- *Female turtles return to lay their eggs on or near the same beach where they hatched.*
- *The sex of baby sea turtles is determined after fertilization by the temperature at which the egg develops (unlike in humans where gender is determined during fertilization).*

from Blue Ridge mountain streams—a habitat for playful river otters—to Coastal Plains, where blackwater swamps harbor such denizens as alligators and diamondback rattlesnakes. Check the day's events for lively demonstrations, animal shows, and informative talks on topics of interest.

The Great Ocean

On the first floor, the aquarium's largest exhibit is two stories tall and contains more than 385,000 gallons of salt water—the water weighs as much as 457 adult African elephants! Watch 450 fish of 50 different species swim by, including a 220-pound loggerhead sea turtle, nurse sharks and porkfish, through a 28-foot-tall acrylic window. Stick around for the daily educational dive shows *(1:30pm, 2:30pm and 3:30pm)*, and animal encounters *(daily 10am and 4pm)*.

Touch Tank

In the aquarium's Touch Tank (on the upper level), kids can have close encounters of the fishy kind with hermit crabs, sea urchins, horseshoe crabs, sea anemones, whelks, sea stars and other creatures called live invertebrates (animals without a backbone) that can be found on South Carolina's coast. Staff members are on hand to answer questions and tell curious youngsters about all these amazing critters.

Zucker Family Sea Turtle Recovery

This new exhibit on the first floor gives visitors a rare look at the workings of the aquarium's sea turtle hospital. Watch actual surgeries through a one-way window, see recovering patients swimming in their tanks, and learn about turtle triage. Turtle Talks are held daily at 11:30am and 2:30pm.

The Shallows

Overlooking the Charleston Harbor from Riverside Terrace, the aquarium's outdoor exhibit invites visitors to have a close encounter with small cownose rays and southern stingrays in an impressive 20,000-gallon touch tank. The Shallows also encompasses a deep area where the animals can swim uninterrupted.

THE CHARLESTON MUSEUM ★

360 Meeting St. - ☎843-722-2996 - www.charlestonmuseum.org - Open year-round Mon-Sat 9am-5pm, Sun noon-5pm - Closed major holidays - $12 adults, $5 children (ages 3-12) - Combination tickets ($25) are available for the museum, the Heyward-Washington and Joseph Manigault house - ♿.

Located across the street from the Visitor Center, exhibits in this contemporary brick structure cover Charleston and the Lowcountry's social and natural history from pre-settlement days to the present. The scope of the museum's holdings ranges from a prehistoric crocodile skeleton to a scale model of a Civil War-era submarine.

Museum Highlights

Lowcountry History Hall – The museum's largest permanent exhibit begins with the area's geology and native inhabitants. It tells the story of Charleston from its first settlers, through the Revolution and the city's plantation heyday, to the Civil War and Reconstruction, and finally to the 20C. Objects like Revolutionary War swords, sweetgrass baskets used to process rice, and Victorian furnishings, illustrate each period in the city's long history.

The Early Days – An Egyptian mummy and taxidermied polar bear may not have much connection to the Lowcountry, but they are among the artifacts from the original museum, which was located in Thompson Auditorium nearby. Founded in 1773, the old museum provided a «window on the world» with its casts of ancient Roman statues, specimens, and skeletons of prehistoric animals.

Loeblein Gallery of Charleston Silver – The museum showcases fine holdings of 18C and 19C silver made in Charleston. George Washington's christening cup is one of the collection's treasures.

DOCK STREET THEATRE ★

135 Church St., at Queen St. - ☎843-577-7183 - www.charlestonstage.com.

Above its recessed porch lined with brownstone columns, this Church Street fixture features a lacy wrought-iron balcony that looks like it belongs in the French Quarter of New Orleans. The original «theatre in Dock Street» opened in 1736, the first structure in the American colonies dedicated solely to the performing arts. The current building, constructed as a hotel in 1809, is the fourth structure on this site. In the 1930s it was renovated as part of a WPA project to function again as a theater.

After 70 years of continuous use, the 462-seat theater recently underwent a multimillion-dollar renovation that restored its historic character and included new dressing rooms and elevators, upgraded wiring and lighting, and seismic reinforcements. Since reopening in spring of 2010, the refurbished theater once again hosts the Spoleto USA Festival (👁see p.130) and other events and continues to serve as the home of the Charleston Stage Company.

GIBBES MUSEUM OF ART ★

135 Meeting St. - ☎843-722-2706 - www.gibbesmuseum.org - Open year-round Tue-Sat 10am-5pm (Wed until 8pm), Sun 1pm-5pm - Closed major holidays - $15 adults, $6 children (ages 4-17) - Café - ♿.

American art with a Charleston perspective—that's what you'll find at the Gibbes. Most of the holdings, which include 10,000 objects, in the 1905 Beaux Arts building showcase works that have some connection to the Lowcountry. Either they were created in Charleston, done by local artists, collected by the city's residents, or portray life in the Charleston area.

The museum reopened in May 2016 following a $17 million renovation and restoration that restored the building's symmetry and exposed some of the original brickwork. It also added 5,000 square feet to the structure's footprint, enabling the museum to display six percent of the collection (as opposed to one percent before the renovation) at any one time. As you enter, you now look straight back to the landscaped **Lenhardt Garden** outside, where a lovely fountain fills a round infinity pool. The first floor holds classrooms, artist-in-residence studios, the gift shop, and the new café, **The Daily by Butcher and Bee**.

The permanent collection is housed on the second floor, while gallery space on the third floor contains changing exhibits, as well as the new glass-walled **storage area**. Periodic tours of this area provide a rare look at how the art is maintained and catalogued.

Permanent Collection Highlights

The rotating permanent collection on the second floor occupies galleries 1-7 and spans four centuries. When you come up the stairs, you'll be in a grand domed rotunda, set about with sculpture and used for special events.

18C and 19C American Paintings and Sculpture

The first in the museum's set of chronologically organized room displays paintings by the likes of Benjamin West, Gilbert Stuart, Thomas Sully, and Henrietta Johnston, who is hailed as America's first professional female artist.

Miniature Portraits

In Gallery 5 you'll find the third-largest collection of its kind in the country, displayed in glass cases and viewable pull-out storage drawers. These examples of tiny paintings from the 18C through the early 20C, conceived as tokens of affection, encompass works by English, French and American artists.

20th Century American Regionalism and the Charleston Renaissance

These galleries hold works by Elizabeth O'Neill Verner, Alice Ravenel Huger Smith, Anna Heyward Taylor and Alfred Huffy. They were part of a small group of artists whose work brought national attention to Charleston's rich cultural heritage during a period dubbed the Charleston Renaissance (1915-40). Alice Smith's Rice **Plantation Series**, original watercolors that she donated to the Gibbes in 1937, are among the museum's most prized works.

Elegant staircase in Joseph Manigault House

33

Jackson Gallery – Named for African-American fiber artist Mary Jackson, this space contains contemporary art by a number of artists, including Jackson's largest sweetgrass basket, titled *Never Again*, as it took her three years to complete.

JOSEPH MANIGAULT HOUSE★

350 Meeting St., at the corner of John St. - ☎843-723-2926 - www.charlestonmuseum.org - Visit by 30-minute guided tour only, year-round Mon-Sat 10am–5pm, Sun noon-5pm - Closed major holidays - $12 - Combination tickets ($25) are available for Heyward-Washington House, Joseph Manigault House and The Charleston Museum.

Gentleman architect **Gabriel Manigault** designed this graceful three-story brick residence, with its distinctive half-moon-shaped piazza (north side), for his brother Joseph in 1803. Located just across the street from The Charleston Museum, the house captures the lifestyle of prosperous early-19C Huguenot rice planters. Typical of the Adam (or Federal) style of architecture—named for English architect Robert Adam—the mansion incorporates a variety of shapes, such as arched doorways,

Four Corners of Law

Originally intended to be a grand public square, the intersection of Broad and Meeting streets holds public buildings on its four corners that each represent a different branch of the law:

- *Completed in 1788, the **Charleston County Court House**, on the northwest corner, exemplifies state law.*
- *The 1896 Renaissance Revival **U.S. Court House and Post Office**, on the southwest corner, represents federal law.*
- *On the northeast corner, Palladian-style **City Hall**, built in 1801, stands in for municipal law.*
- ***St. Michael's Episcopal Church★**, which graces the southeast corner, represents God's law.*

fanlights and a sinuous **staircase★★**. Throughout the residence, you'll see delicately carved woodwork, another earmark of the Adam style, as well as a group of French, English and American 19C furniture from The Charleston Museum's fine collection.

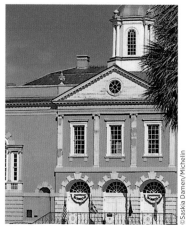
Old Exchange Building

OLD EXCHANGE BUILDING AND PROVOST DUNGEON★

122 E. Bay St., at Broad St. - ☎843-727-2165 - oldexchange.org - Open year-round daily 9am-5pm - Closed Jan 1, Thanksgiving Day and Dec 25 - $10 - ♿ (call ahead).

The Old Exchange Building was the city's commercial, political and social hub in the late 18C. Constructed in 1771 on the site of Half-Moon Bastion—part of the original fortifications around the city—the Georgian-style Exchange and Custom House, with its arched Palladian windows and distinctive cupola, was the last structure that the British erected in Charleston. Soon after its completion, the Exchange received George Washington, who visited Charleston in May 1771. An elaborate dinner was served to him in the 4,000-square-foot first-floor arcade, followed by a grand ball.

The Exchange is one of only three buildings in the country where the

34

©Saskia Damen/Michelin

US Constitution was ratified in 1788 (the other two were Independence Hall in Philadelphia and Faneuil Hall in Boston). Some of the very men who signed the document had been imprisoned downstairs in the damp, gloomy Provost Dungeon during the British occupation. Displays detail the building's history, especially its connection to America's fight for independence.

Provost Dungeon – *Visit by 20-minute guided tour only.* Kids will enjoy the spooky dungeon, constructed of brick in 1781 with a barrel-vaulted ceiling and thick columns. Located in the basement of the Old Exchange Building, the dungeon was opened as a museum in 1966. Today it is outfitted with animatronic figures representing characters from the city's past, who tell their woeful tales. Some prominent citizens were held here, charged by the British with giving intelligence to the Patriots. This is the one place in town where you can see part of the **original seawall** built in the late 17C to fortify the city.

WATERFRONT PARK★

1 Vendue Range, from Cumberland St. to Tradd St. - ☎843-724-7321 - www. charlestonparksconservancy.org.
Set along Charleston Harbor, in the Historic District, this 12-acre linear park occupies the space once filled by the old port's wharves. A fanciful **pineapple fountain** marks its center. In warm weather (which is most of the

© Brigitta L. House/Michelin

Waterfront Park

White Point Gallows

*In its early days, Charles Towne was plagued by pirates, including the notorious **Edward Teach**, aka "Blackbeard," who captured several ships in Charleston Harbor in 1718. Perhaps Charleston's most famous rogue was Stede Bonnet, the well-educated son of a wealthy Barbadian family who turned to piracy after serving as a major in the Barbados army. Whether Bonnet became a pirate to escape his wife's incessant nagging, as legend has it, or whether his whim "proceeded from a disorder of his mind," as his cronies believed, remains anyone's guess.*

Called "the gentleman pirate" for his cultured manner, Bonnet took part in Blackbeard's siege of Charleston Harbor. In 1718 Bonnet was captured on the Cape Fear River in North Carolina and brought back to Charleston to stand trial for his crimes. Despite his gentlemanly behavior, Bonnet was sentenced to hang in White Point Gardens—along with 49 other pirates who met the same fate later that year (Bonnet's letter pleading for his life is on display in the Old Provost Dungeon. A plaque in the park commemorates Bonnet and the other pirates who met their end in White Point Gardens.

year in Charleston) kids love to run through the circular fountain by the pier (at the end of Vendue Range). Joggers and walkers favor the paved walkway that hugs the waterfront, and the park's spacious green lawns make a great place for a picnic. On the inland side of the park, small landscaped garden rooms provide peaceful nooks for outdoor reading. At the end of Vendue Range, a 400-foot **pier** juts into the harbor. Bring your rod and reel, or just claim one of the wooden swings and enjoy the view.

Keeper of the Gates

*In Charleston's Historic District, the wrought- and cast-ironwork that adorns many of the garden gates rivals New Orleans in this decorative art form, which evolved from 19C plantation blacksmiths who made and repaired tools. The best examples of this art were fashioned by Charleston's favorite son, **Philip Simmons** (1912–2009), known world-wide for his decorative ironwork. Simmons was born on nearby Daniel Island, and his work appears in some 500 gates, balconies and fences throughout the district. In 1982 Simmons was named a National Folk Treasure by the Smithsonian and the National Park Service when one of his gates was displayed at the Smithsonian Institution's National Museum of American History in Washington, DC. After his death at age 97, his home was turned into a museum (30-1/2 Blake St. - 843-723-1259 - www.philipsimmons.us - open Tue-Sat 11am-4pm).*

WHITE POINT GARDENS ★

Along the Battery, at the intersection of E. Bay St. and Murray Blvd. - ✆843-724-7327 - www. charlestonparksconservancy.org.
Named for the gleaming white oyster beds that the first settlers found on this site in 1670, White Point occupies the southern tip of Charleston's peninsula. It was here that the settlers relocated their fledgling town in 1680. This strategic point at the junction of the Ashley and Cooper rivers was used to defend the city as far back as the early 1700s, when the original walls were built around the new town. Established as a public park in 1837, White Point was again used as a gun battery during the Civil War.

A number of Confederate cannons still stand in the park as reminders of less peaceful times. Monuments here honor heroes from the Revolutionary and Civil wars, including the crew of the H.L. Hunley (👁*see p 65*).
The gracious four-block-long park was laid out in 1906 by John Charles Olmsted (stepson of the renowned landscape architect Frederick Law Olmsted, whose credits include New York's Central Park). Also referred to simply as The Battery, White Point Gardens makes a wonderful spot for strolling, picnicking or just relaxing amid its palmettos and moss-draped live oak trees. Of course, the expansive view river is not bad, either. You can even see Fort Sumter in the distance (look for the flagpole).

White Point Gardens

CHILDREN'S MUSEUM OF THE LOWCOUNTRY

25 Ann St., behind the Charleston Visitor Center on Meeting St. - ☎843-853-8962 - explorecml.org - Open year-round Tue-Sat 9am-5pm, Sun noon-5pm - Closed Mon and major holidays - $12 ($10 for SC residents), free for children under 12 months - &.
From toddler to age 10, kids will find a lot of activity in store at the Children's Museum. With a mission to engage young children's potential by inviting families of all backgrounds to explore environments and experiences that spark imagination and stimulate curiosity through the power of play, the museum exposes youngsters to the arts, sciences and humanities through a series of exhibits and play stations. Kids can dress up as a medieval monarch in the two-story **Medieval Creativity Castle**; create their own rain storm in **WaterWise**; design, build, and take toys apart in **Idea Factory**; and explore their creativity in **The Art Room**. In **Pirates!**, children delight in donning pirate hats and brandishing mock swords aboard a pirate ship, while learning to tie knots like a seasoned sailor. Don't worry, the kids won't realize it's all educational—they'll just think it's fun!

CONFEDERATE MUSEUM

188 Meeting St., at the corner of Market St. - ☎843-723-1541 - www.confederatemuseumcharlestonsc.com - Open year-round Tue-Sat 11am-3:30pm - Closed Sun, Mon and major holidays - $5 - &.
Established by the Daughters of the Confederacy in 1898, this collection on the second floor of Market Hall contains an important group of artifacts and archives of documents from the Civil War, including uniforms, weapons, flags and historic photographs.

HIBERNIAN HALL

105 Meeting St. - Not open to the public.
Built in 1840, this National Historic Landmark was—and still is—the meeting place for the Ancient Order of Hibernians, an Irish Catholic organization whose members are devoted to the welfare of their fellow

©Doug Rogers/Michelin

Hibernian Hall

Irishmen. Hibernian Hall's claim to historical fame is the fact that it hosted the National Democratic Convention of 1860 for the party faction supporting Stephen A. Douglas to run against Abraham Lincoln. The hall is pure Greek Revival in style, designed by Philadelphia architect Thomas U. Walter, whose work includes an expansion of the Capitol in Washington, DC. Notice the harp carved above the main door and incorporated into the iron entrance gate. This motif echoes the Irish heritage of the hall's founders.

OLD SLAVE MART MUSEUM

6 Chalmers St. - ☎843-958-6467 - oldslavemartmuseum.com - Open year-round Mon-Sat 9am-pm - Closed Jan 1, Thanksgiving Day and Dec 25 - $8 adults, $5 children - ♿.
Now tucked away on a residential street, the slave mart opened in 1856 when the practice of selling slaves publicly on the side of the Custom House (now the Old Exchange Building) was outlawed. In the 18C, Charleston was the main port of entry for the American slave trade. The last auction was held here in 1863.
In 1938 the building was opened as a museum showcasing African arts and crafts, and operated until 1987, when the city took over the property. Renovated and reopened in 2007, the museum retains the high-arched entrance of the original mart, which once featured octagonal pillars and an iron gate. Exhibits in the ground-floor room, which served as the salesroom, call attention to a dark period in of American history.

POWDER MAGAZINE

79 Cumberland St. - ☎843-722-9350 - www.powdermag.org - Open year-round Mon-Sat 10am-4pm, Sun 1pm-4pm - $6 adults, $3 children - ♿.
Understandably, here are few structures that survive today from the days when Charleston was the domain of the Lord Proprietors appointed by King Charles II. The windowless, tile-roof Powder Magazine, completed in 1713, is one of them. Inside its 32-inch-thick walls, soldiers stored munitions and gunpowder used to defend the fortified city against attack from Spanish troops, hostile Indians and marauding pirates. (The cannons out front aren't quite that old; they date from the Revolutionary War.) It's worth your time to walk through the oldest public building in the city, where you'll find an interactive exhibit that tells the story of Charleston's earliest days.

U.S. CUSTOM HOUSE

200 E. Bay St. - Not open to the public.
The stately white United States Custom House lords it over East Bay Street at the foot of Market Street. Shaped in a cross, the monumental structure is fronted by massive Corinthian columns and measures 259 feet on its east-west axis and 152 feet on its north-south axis. Construction began in 1853, but engineering problems, lack of funding, and damage caused by the intervening

Civil War delayed its completion until 1879. Ever since then, it has operated as a United States Customs facility.

HISTORIC SYNAGOGUE AND CHURCHES

Unlike Boston and Philadelphia, which were founded by Puritans and Quakers respectively, Charleston wasn't settled by any one religious group. Although the Anglican Church of England was predominant in the early city, Charleston promoted religious tolerance, and provided places of worship for many different beliefs. The spires of myriad churches are still visible across the peninsula today, giving rise to Charleston's nickname, The Holy City.

French Huguenot Church

© Saskia Damen/Michelin

Here are some of the most historic of the peninsula's 180 churches:

Kahal Kadosh Beth Elohim Synagogue

90 Hasell St. - ☎843-723-1090 - www. kkbe.org. Tours ($10) Mon-Fri 10:15am, 11:15am, 1:15pm and 2:15pm - ♿.
Built in 1840 (the congregation was organized in 1749), this impressive Classical Revival-style National Historic Landmark is the second-oldest synagogue in the US, and the oldest one still in use. The American Reform Judaism Movement was born here in 1842.

Circular Congregational Church★★

150 Meeting St. - ☎843-577-6400 - www.circularcongreagational church.org - ♿. Designed by Charleston architect Robert Mills, this striking brick Romanesque Revival church stands on the site of the first Independent Church, or Church for Dissenters (non-Anglicans), founded in 1681. The original circular church was built here in 1806. It burned in 1861 and its ruins fell during the 1886 earthquake. The graveyard you see now, the city's oldest, dates to 1695.

First (Scots) Presbyterian Church★

53 Meeting St. - ☎843-722-8882 - www.first-scots.org - Tours after Sun service at 8:45am and 11:15am - ♿.
You'll recognize the stucco-covered First Presbyterian Church (1814) by its columned Greek Revival facade and by the twin rounded towers that top its roof. This congregation was formed in 1731, when 12 Scottish

St. Philip's Churchyard

The two sections of St. Philip's churchyard (east and west) hold the graves of some of the city's most prominent citizens and historical figures, including South Carolina statesman and secessionist John C. Calhoun, Edward Rutledge, a signer of the Declaration of Independence, and author and playwright Dubose Heyward.

families left the Independent Church and started their own meeting house, the Scots Kirk. Out front, the wrought-iron gates incorporate a motif of thistles, the symbol of Scotland.

French Huguenot Church★

136 Church St. - 📞843-722-4385 - www.huguenot-church.net - ♿.
Seeking to escape religious persecution in France, French Protestants, called Huguenots, came to Charleston beginning in the late

17C. The first church they built was destroyed by fire in 1796. The 1845 church, the third built on this site, was the first Gothic Revival structure in the city. Its original pipe organ still provides music during services.

St. Michael's Episcopal Church★

71 Broad St. - 📞843-723-0603 - stmichaelschurch.net.
George Washington might not have slept here, but he did worship in this 1761 Colonial-style church.

41

©Tetra Images/hemis.fr

St. Philip's Episcopal Church

Representing divine law on the intersection known as the Four Corners of Law (◐see p. 35), St. Michael's sits on the site of Charleston's original Anglican Church. Its 186-foot-tall steeple was used as a Revolutionary War lookout tower, and as a signal tower during the Civil War.

Emanuel A.M.E. Church

110 Calhoun St. - ✆843-722-2561 - www.emanuelamechurch.org - ♿.
The oldest black congregation south of Baltimore, Maryland, attends services at Emanuel African Methodist Episcopal Church. Built in 1891, the Gothic-style church boasts a Victorian interior that retains its original altar, pews and light fixtures.

First Baptist Church

61 Church St. - ✆843-722-3896 - www.fbcharleston.org - Sanctuary tours Mon-Fri 9am-2pm (check in at office, 48 Meeting St.) - ♿.
Designed by Charleston architect Robert Mills, the 1822 First Baptist Church reigns as the oldest Baptist church in the South. The original congregation was organized in Maine in 1692.

St. John's Lutheran Church

– 5 Clifford St. - ✆843-723-2426 - stjohnscharleston.org - ♿.
Charleston's oldest Lutheran congregation dates to 1742, but their first church wasn't completed until 1818. Added in 1859, the steeple with its bell-shaped top may have been the design of Charles Fraser, a Charleston architect and painter.

St. Mary's Roman Catholic Church

89 Hasell St. - ✆843-329-3237 - stmaryshasellst.org - ♿. Organized in 1789, the first Roman Catholic church in the southeastern US had a large French congregation. Walk through the churchyard and notice that many of the gravestones are in French. The present Classical Revival church building was completed in 1839 to replace a brick building that burned down the previous year.

St. Philip's Episcopal Church

142 Church St. - ✆843-722-7734 - www.stphilipschurchsc.org - ♿. Organized in 1680, St. Philip's was founded the year the colonists moved to the peninsula from swampy Charles Towne. The present church dates to 1838. Its lofty eight-sided steeple once held a light that guided sailors to Charleston's port.

DRAYTON HALL ★★★

3380 Ashley River Rd. - ✆843-769-2600 - www.draytonhall.org - Visit by 1-hour guided tour only, year-round Mon-Sat 9am-5pm (last tour at 3:30pm), Sun 11am-5pm - Closed Jan 1 and Dec 24, 25 and 31 - $22 - $12 grounds only.
Considered to be one of the finest existing examples of Georgian-Palladian architecture in America, Drayton Hall is the only plantation house on the Ashley River to have survived the Revolutionary and Civil wars intact. No one knows how for sure, but one story goes that the slaves remaining at the house put up yellow flags to indicate an

© R. Ellis/age fotostock

Drayton Hall

43

outbreak of deadly yellow fever on-site to ward off Union troops. Another theory holds that the son on the Union side (the family was divided during the war, with one son fighting for the Union Army and the rest for the Confederates) used his influence to convince Yankee officers to spare his home. Like their relatives at nearby Magnolia Plantation, the Draytons weathered the poverty of the Reconstruction years by mining phosphate (for fertilizer) on their land. Begun in 1738 and completed in 1742 for John Drayton, the majestic brick mansion—whose architect is unknown—overlooks the river from its 125-acre site. Symmetry and

To the Manor Born: The Drayton Family

Descended from Norman aristocracy, ancestors of the modern-day Drayton family made their way to England via Aubrey de Vere, who came with William the Conqueror in 1066. After distinguishing himself during the Battle of Hastings, de Vere was awarded a Saxon castle in Northampton, known as Drayton House (de Vere later took the name of this property). The first Draytons to come to America–Thomas and his son, Thomas Jr. (⚓see p. 42) —began a long line of that family in the mid-1600s, many of whom became prominent figures in American politics. John Drayton, who built Drayton Hall, was born next door at Magnolia Plantation in 1715.

44

Touring Tip

If you buy tickets to Drayton Hall online, you're not guaranteed a specific date or tour time. When you present your pre-paid tickets on-site, you'll be added to the first available tour (filled on a first-come, first-served basis).

classical detail distinguish the 2-story, 10-room interior, which remains in near original condition. The raised English basement was used largely for storage space. Two 2-story brick outbuildings, known as flankers, were constructed in the 18C, one to serve as a kitchen and the other as a laundry space. One flanker was lost in the 1886 earthquake; the kitchen flanker was destroyed by an 1893 hurricane. Only the privy building, once containing seven seats, remains from the 18C. It was converted to an office in the late 19C.

Royal Judge John Drayton used his country home for lavish entertaining and as a base from which to manage his other estates. At his death, Drayton ranked as one of the wealthiest men in the Carolina colony. In 1780 British troops seized the house, which became the headquarters for British commander Sir Henry Clinton, and later for British General Charles Cornwallis. Thousands of Redcoats camped on the grounds. The mansion later served as headquarters for the Continental Army during the British occupation of Charleston. The home was occupied by seven generations of the Drayton family before 1969, when it passed into the hands of the National Trust for Historic Preservation, which operates this valuable National Historic Landmark today.

Hall Highlights

Begin your visit at the new **Visitor Center**, which provides an orientation to the house and displays a small part of Drayton Hall's fine collection of furniture and historical artifacts connected with the property. Inside the home you'll find no furnishings—those were sold at auction long ago—but you will see a wealth of ornate hand-carved and cast-plaster ceilings and hand-carved decorative moldings. The last finished coat of paint on the walls dates to 1885.

Grand entrance – Note that the entrance to Drayton Hall faced the river, since most 18C and 19C guests arrived by boat.

Portico – The massive, two-story portico on the front side facing the road was reputedly the first of its kind in the colonies. Just inside, the 27-foot-high entry hall shows off a mahogany **double staircase** with newel posts.

Upstairs hall – The Draytons used this space for formal dining, dances and other social events. Doors here open onto the second story of the portico.

Drawing Room – Downstairs, the Drawing Room boasts a gorgeous ornate ceiling that was hand-molded in wet plaster.

Drayton Hall

Ashley River Road Plantations★★★

Charleston's plantations hark back to an era when rice flourished in flooded land along the rivers, providing riches for plantation owners and exhausting work for their slaves. Meandering up the south side of the Charleston peninsula, the Ashley River served in colonial times as the main route to the plantations that lined its banks. By land, an arduous back road traced part of an ancient Cherokee Indian trail. Today, tree-lined Ashley River Road (Route 61) provides easy access to three stellar plantations.

▶**Tip:** If you don't have a car, you can get a taxi, Lyft or Uber (both average about $24) to the plantations or take one of the plantation tours that depart from the Charleston Visitors Center at 375 Meeting St.

MIDDLETON PLACE★★★

46

4300 Ashley River Rd. - ☏843-556-6020 - www.middletonplace.org - Open year-round daily 9am-5pm - Closed Dec 25 - Admission (gardens and stableyards) $28 adults, $10 children (free for children under age 6) - Combination tickets available for gardens, carriage ride and house tour: $55 adults, $39 children - Restaurant - ♿.

Touring Tip

Middleton's $28 admission fee includes the stableyards and gardens but not the house tour ($15). The stableyards and gardens are all walkable. If you want to see some areas outside the main plantation grounds, you can take a 45-minute carriage ride ($18, in addition to admission fee).

The land that came to Englishman Henry Middleton as part of his wife's dowry in 1741 now sweeps down to the Ashley River in 110 acres of green terraced lawns and symmetrical 18C English gardens. Laid out in 1741 by Henry Middleton, the gardens once formed part of the Middleton rice plantation. If all this seems like too much to see in one day, make reservations at the Inn at Middleton Place (☞see p. 139)

Gardens★★★

Complimentary 30-minute garden tours offered daily on the hour, 10am-3pm (depart from the Greensward near the Ruins). America owes its oldest landscaped gardens to moneyed plantation owner Henry Middleton, who laid them out in classic European style in 1741. More than 100 slaves spent 10 years digging ornamental canals, planting shrubs and forming the land to Middleton's

A Muster of Middletons

The Middletons exerted their fair share of influence in American politics.

Henry Middleton *(1717–1784)* – *By the time of the Revolution, Henry owned 50,000 acres of land and 800 slaves. He was elected president of the First Continental Congress in 1774.*

Arthur Middleton *(1743–1787)* – *The eldest of Henry's five sons was one of the signers of the Declaration of Independence in 1776.*

Henry Middleton *(1770–1846)* – *Henry's grandson and Arthur's eldest son served as governor of South Carolina from 1810 to 1812 and as ambassador to Russia during the 1820s.*

Williams Middleton *(1809–1883)* – *Henry's great-grandson (son of the second Henry) signed the Ordinance of Secession. His staunch support of the Confederate cause spurred Union troops to destroy his family's home in 1865.*

elaborate plan. In keeping with 18C ideals of a garden, his plan called for symmetrical galleries walled in by greenery, and views reaching down to the river across wide, grassy lawns.

The main sight line slopes down from the entrance gates over terraces above the twin butterfly lakes (shaped like two butterfly wings) to the Ashley River just beyond. Opened

© Middleton Place, Charleston, South Carolina

Aerial view of Middleton Place Gardens

©Middleton Place, Charleston, South Carolina

Main Room, House Museum, Middleton Place

to the public in the 1920s, Middleton's masterpiece has been added to over the years. New plantings now color the original plan, so the gardens bloom 12 months of the year.

House Museum

Visit by 45min guided tour only, Mon noon-4:30pm, Tue-Sun 10am-4:30pm (hours vary seasonally) - $15 (free for children under age 5). Built as a gentleman's guest quarters in 1755, this brick dwelling is all that survives of the grand three-building complex that the Middleton family called home. The parts of the complex that weren't destroyed by the Union Army in 1865 toppled in the 1886 earthquake. Inside are fine family furnishings and memorabilia.

Camellias

Middleton Place sponsors special guided walks that spotlight its prized collection of lovely camellias. Of the 4,000 camellias planted here, the oldest dates back to 1786. Tours last 1.5 hours and are held on selected days (Feb-late Mar: Tue, Thu & Sat) at 11am. Reservations are required.

Mill House

Positioned at the edge of the mill pond, the brick mill building across from the twin butterfly lakes today houses an exhibit on colonial rice production. Gracing the walls are exquisite watercolors, painted by Alice Ravenel Huger Smith (1876–1958), that illustrate the process.

Stableyards

Visit the stableyards to see behind the scenes of a working colonial plantation. You'll find heritage breeds here, along with artisans who demonstrate such essential skills as weaving, carpentry and blacksmithing.

MAGNOLIA PLANTATION AND GARDENS ★★

3550 Ashley River Rd. - ✆843-571-1266 - www.magnoliaplantation.com - Open mid-Mar–Oct daily 8am-5:30pm - Rest of the year daily 8:30am-4:30pm - $20 adults, $10 children (ages 6-12) - Café.
Home to 13 generations of the Drayton family, Magnolia Plantation has been open to the public since shortly after the Civil War, and is still owned by the family that created it. Magnolia's story begins in the mid-1600s, when an Englishman named Stephen Fox left Barbados for Charleston, where he acquired a 500-acre tract of land on the Ashley River (later named Magnolia Plantation). About the same time, Thomas Drayton, another wealthy Barbadian, came to town with his son, Thomas Jr. As it happened, Thomas Jr. ended up marrying Stephen Fox's daughter, Ann, who came into the family with the plantation site as her dowry. Thomas built the original house at Magnolia Plantation, and the Drayton family has operated the estate ever since.

In 1820 the estate came into the hands of 22-year-old John Grimke Drayton, who later became a minister. Rev. Drayton developed the striking informal gardens here to comfort his wife, Julia, who was homesick for her native city of Philadelphia.

Gardens ★★

Azaleas rule. At least they do at Magnolia's 50 acres of gardens from mid-March through April, when some 250 different varieties of azaleas paint the canal banks in vibrant pink, white and purple. After Rev. John Grimke Drayton inherited Magnolia Plantation in 1820, he developed the existing gardens, enhancing the natural

For the Birders

Sunday mornings at 8:30am, Magnolia Plantation sponsors a guided bird walk. Among the 254 species that have been spotted here, you might see great blue herons, coots, anhingas, egrets, gallinules and bald eagles during the 2.5-hour tour (bring binoculars and bug spray). Ask at the admissions gate for the walk's starting point. Tickets ($22) include admission to the garden and grounds.

© H. Looney / DanitaDelimont.com/ age fotostock

Long white bridge, Magnolia Plantation

landscape, rather than creating a formal garden such as the one at Middleton Place. He is credited with introducing the first *Azalea Indica* to America in the mid-19C.

© Brigitta L. House/Michelin

Anhinga in Magnolia Plantation

Today spring brings twisting wisteria vines dripping with clusters of lavender flowers, delicate yellow forsythia, fragrant honeysuckle and pink and white dogwoods—so don't forget your camera! In summer you'll find magnolias along with lilies and wildflowers. In fall and winter some 900 types of camellias burst into bloom. More than 150 of them were developed on the plantation. Garden highlights include the graceful **Long White Bridge**, which Rev. Drayton built in the 1840s to span a natural river marsh. Plants that might have grown in the Garden of Eden grace the **Biblical Garden**, while the **Barbados Tropical Garden** displays flora from the island home of the plantation's original owner. Kids and adults will love getting lost in the

maze, a labyrinth of camellias and hollies modeled on the boxwood maze that King Henry VIII designed for his country estate in the 16C.

AUDUBON SWAMP GARDENS ★★

At Magnolia Gardens - $8 with paid Magnolia Garden admission (children under age 6 free. Be sure to bring bug spray in warm weather—especially summer—to keep the mosquitos away in this swampy setting.

Covering an eerie 60 acres of blackwater cypress and tupelo swamp, this area was added to Magnolia Plantation in the 1980s. It takes its name from early-19C naturalist John James Audubon, who visited Magnolia Plantation to study waterbirds during one of his many trips to Charleston.

Allow at least an hour to wander the boardwalks and bridges through the

Swamp Thing

The murky water of Audubon Swamp Garden made a fitting setting for the 1982 horror flick The Swamp Thing, starring Louis Jourdan and Adrienne Barbeau.

swamp and give yourself ample time to take in the colors and textures, such as brilliant green duckweed that makes the water appear solid, the knobby black silhouettes of cypress knees, lacy ferns and bright lilies. Keep your eye out for wildlife along the way. White ibis, blue-winged teals, great blue herons and snowy egrets are just a sampling of the more than 200 types of birds that have been spotted here. Otters, turtles and, of course, alligators are ever-present denizens of the swamp.

51

©NDJordan/Michelin

Alligator sunning

Around the Charleston Area

Not everything worth seeing in Charleston is in the Historic District. Venturing out a bit farther afield is equally rewarding in terms of historic sites, be it to Charles Towne Landing, where the first English colonists dropped anchor or to see the remains of the vessel that was responsible for the world's first successful submarine attack. Across the Cooper River in Mt. Pleasant, you can visit sites that preserve Revolutionary War battles and World War II battleships. And don't miss a cruise out to Fort Sumter★★★, where the first shots of the Civil War were fired.

▶**Tip:** Organize your visit to sights that are in the same area and make a day of it. Check out the restaurant section in Addresses for suggested places for lunch.

FORT SUMTER NATIONAL MONUMENT★★★

Accessible only by boat from Patriots Point or the Fort Sumter Visitor Education Center, located on Liberty Square (next to the SC Aquarium at Calhoun and Concord Sts.) - ✆843-883-3123 - www.nps.gov/fosu - Open mid-Mar-Labor Day 9:30am-5pm (last boat from Liberty Square leaves at 4pm; last boat from Patriots Point leaves at 3:30pm; pack long sleeves for the wind!) - Rest of the year, call

Touring Tip

Allow at least two hours—you could easily spend longer—to explore the Yorktown and the other ships. Scrambling up and down through the decks of the Yorktown can be tricky. Climbing up and down the ladder-like stairways (elevators are also available) between the ship's decks requires a certain amount of agility.

Getting to Fort Sumter

Fort Sumter Tours offers the only authorized boat transportation to Fort Sumter. Boats depart from the Fort Sumter Visitor Education Center on Liberty Square, and from Patriots Point Naval Maritime Museum (☾see p. 52) in Mt. Pleasant. On the 30-minute narrated cruise, you'll learn about events leading to the war. Allow 2.5hrs to visit the fort, including the boat trip. For boat schedules, call ✆843-722-2628 or ✆800-789-3678 - fortsumtertours.com - $22 adults, $14 children (under age 3 ride free).

Courtesy of the National Park Service

Fort Sumter parade ground prior to the April 1861 bombardment, as published in Harper's Weekly February 16, 1861

for hours - Closed Jan 1, Thanksgiving Day and Dec 25 - Fee for cruise includes admission to fort. ♿ (except for the upper levels of the fort).
Imagine this lonely outpost at the entrance to Charleston Harbor alive with cannon fire, men running and shouting, the powder magazines exploding in flames. This was the scene on April 12, 1861, when Confederate forces fired the first shots of the Civil War.

When South Carolina seceded from the Union on December 20, 1860, four forts guarded the entrance to Charleston Harbor: Fort Sumter on its man-made island, Fort Moultrie on Sullivans Island, Fort Johnson on James Island, and Castle Pinckney

Fort Fun Facts

- It took seven million bricks to build Fort Sumter.
- The outer walls of the fort were five feet thick.
- The fort's three tiers rose 50 feet above water level.
- Designed for a garrison of 650 men, the fort could bear an armament of 135 guns.

on Shutes Folly Island. The five-sided brick fort, named for South Carolina Revolutionary War hero Thomas Sumter, was 90 percent complete at the time, but only 15 of the fort's

Palmetto Flag, Palmetto State

Why is South Carolina's state flag decorated with a palmetto tree? The design derives from the one that graced the flag carried by South Carolina's Palmetto Guard. Members of the unit planted this standard on Fort Sumter's parapet in April 1861, when Confederate troops took Fort Sumter. Adopted in January 1861, the flag bears a palmetto tree to honor the soft palmetto logs that absorbed enemy shells and saved Fort Moultrie from British attack in 1776. Since 1861, South Carolina has been known as the Palmetto State.

more than 100 cannons stood mounted and ready.

On December 26, Union major Robert Anderson secretly relocated his cadre of 85 men from Fort Moultrie to Fort Sumter—a move that South Carolina responded to by demanding the evacuation of Charleston Harbor by U.S. Government forces. Over the ensuing months, government attempts to resupply the fort led to increasing tensions between the North and South.

A final government effort to get supplies through to Sumter in April 1861 prompted General P.G.T. Beauregard, commander of the Confederate troops in Charleston, to ask Major Anderson to surrender the stronghold. When Anderson refused, Confederate officers informed him that their forces would open fire in an hour. At 3:30am on April 12, 1861, the Rebels fired on Sumter. The cannonade continued for 34 hours, until Major Anderson finally surrendered the fort on April 13. "The firing of the mortar woke the echoes from every nook and corner of the harbour…," wrote Stephen Lee, aide-de-camp to General Beauregard, who commanded the Confederate forces. "A thrill went through the whole city. It was felt that the Rubicon was passed…"

After the Civil War ended in 1865, Fort Sumter stood neglected until 1898, when it was used during the Spanish-American War. The fort was decommissioned in 1947 and transferred to the National Park Service the following year.

Fort Sumter Visitor Education Center

Next to the SC Aquarium - ☎843-577-0242 - Open year-round daily 8:30am -5pm - Closed Jan 1, Thanksgiving, Dec 25. This is the place to purchase tickets for the boat trip to the fort. Displays detail the events leading up to the first shots of the Civil War. Artifacts here include Major Anderson's original garrison flag that once waved over Fort Sumter.

Fort Sumter Walking Tour

Once at the fort, you can inspect the casemates and the ruins of the barracks and officers' quarters on the self-guided walking tour. A museum in Battery Huger, added in 1899, tells the story of the fort and its role in the Civil War through informative panels, armaments and artifacts.

Carolina Gold

Luckily for the area's early economy, rice was well-suited to the Lowcountry's hot, humid climate. The crop first appeared in South Carolina during colonial times from Africa and Indonesia (no one has been able to trace its exact origin.) Slaves from the Rice Coast of West Africa brought their knowledge of how to plant and grow rice to America. With its golden hull and fine quality, this particular variety of African long-grain rice became known as "Carolina Gold." Shipped to markets throughout Europe, rice ruled as South Carolina's most important product up until the Civil War.

Although the colonists' first attempts at growing rice failed, by 1726 the crop was being grown near tidal rivers where fields could be flooded and later drained. It wasn't easy to cultivate rice. Nearly every task associated with rice growing had to be done by hand, from clearing the land to digging the dikes and ditches that would divert river water to the fields, and milling the rice itself.

These tasks fell to the slaves, who served as the backbone of the plantations. In the mid-18C, slaves were expected to clear 1,200 square feet of land a day and hand-thresh 600 sheaves of rice. Using sticks called flails, they beat the rice stalks until the grains fell out; then they separated the grains from the shafts by shaking them in large, flat winnowing baskets. Rice was milled by hand using a mortar and pestle to remove the outer husk.

For nearly 200 years, the 300-mile coastline from Cape Fear, North Carolina, to the St. Marys River in Georgia, reigned as the Kingdom of Rice. In the years before the Civil War, South Carolina counted 227 plantations—70,000 acres of land—in cultivation, which produced an average of 11 million pounds of rice a year. In the late 18C, the wealthy class in Charles Towne was so crazy about rice that local cabinetmakers created the rice bed, carved with rice ears and leaves on its bedposts —a style that's still reproduced today.

Their fortunes assured by the 1840s, rice-plantation owners became gentlemen of leisure, spending much of their time socializing in their Charleston town houses, and managing their estates from afar. After the Civil War, planters couldn't afford to pay workers to do the back-breaking labor that growing rice required. Without free labor, it was too costly to cultivate rice, so planters turned to other means of support, such as growing cotton and mining phosphate along the rivers.

You can purchase certified Carolina Gold plantation rice today at shops throughout the Lowcounty.

© Patriots Point Naval & Maritime Museum

USS Yorktown, The Fighting Lady

PATRIOTS POINT NAVAL AND MARITIME MUSEUM★★

40 Patriots Point Rd., Mt. Pleasant. 3mi north of Charleston via take US-17 North across the bridge to Rte. 703 (first right on Patriots Point Rd.) -

Ghostly Yorktown

The Fighting Lady holds many mysteries, and you can explore them on this 90-minute guided walking tour. Along the way, you'll hear stories of the ship's heroes that still walk these decks and be treated to tales of the strange activity that has been documented on board over the years. Check online for schedule: yorktownghosttours.com.

℘843-884-2727 - www.patriots point.org - Open year-round daily 9am-6:30pm - Closed Dec 25 - $22 adults, $14 children (ages 6-11) - children under age 6 free - Parking $5 - Café - ♿.

You may have wondered what that huge gray shape is across the harbor from Charleston. It's the World War II aircraft carrier the **USS Yorktown★★**, the centerpiece of Patriots Point exhibits. Built to honor the men and women who served in the US Navy in the 20C, Patriots Point features three historic vessels, a mock-up of a US Navy base camp in Vietnam, the Medal of Honor Museum and the Cold War Submarine Memorial (across the parking lot on Charleston Harbor). Dubbed "The Fighting Lady", the

Yorktown was commissioned in Newport News, Virginia, in 1943. During World War II, the aircraft carrier transported a crew of 380 officers and 3,038 enlisted men, along with 90 aircraft on board. After the war she served in Vietnam, and later recovered the astronauts from Apollo 8 when they returned from their moon orbit in 1968. The *Yorktown* was decommissioned in 1970, and the ship was towed from New Jersey to Charleston five years later.

You're free to roam this vast, 888-foot-long floating museum from engine room to bridge, following any of six self-guided tours *(or rent the audio tour for $6)* that take you through five lower decks and seven levels above the hangar bay. In all you'll find 25 naval aircraft on board, some in the hangar bay, others up on the flight deck.

Two additional World War II ships are berthed at Patriots Point: the **USS Clamagore** World War II submarine, and the **USS Laffey** DD724 Destroyer.

CHARLES PINCKNEY NATIONAL HISTORIC SITE ★

1254 Long Point Rd., Mt. Pleasant, 7mi north of Charleston via US-17 North - ☎843-881-5516 - www.nps.gov/chpi - Open year-round daily 9am–5pm - Closed Jan 1, Thanksgiving Day and Dec 25 - ♿.

Patriot and planter Charles Pinckney inherited this Lowcountry estate from his father in 1782. Dubbed Snee Farm, the plantation was Pinckney's favorite "country seat", among the many properties owned by his influential

Courtesy of the National Park Service

Charles Pinckney National Historic Site

family. Pinckney, who spent much time away from the plantation seeing to affairs of state, was forced to sell the farm in 1817 to settle his debts. Today only 28 of the property's original 715 acres remain undeveloped. Although no structures are left from the time when the Pinckneys lived here, the one-and-a-half-story cypress and pine cottage illustrates the type of modest, yet comfortable, dwelling built by Lowcountry planters who spent most of their time in their more opulent town houses in Charleston.

57

Money-saving Touring Tip

If you're on a budget, note that Snee Farm is the only Charleston area plantation with free admission. Take 20 minutes to watch the informative video (shown in the cottage) that details the history of Snee Farm and its owner, Charles Pinckney.

Constitution Charlie

*An often forgotten founding father and son of a wealthy planter, **Charles Cotesworth Pinckney** (1746-1825) is one of four Charlestonians who went to Philadelphia in May 1787 to help draft the new Constitution of the United States. Prior to leaving, Pinckney and John Rutledge wrote a version of the Constitution, which they later presented to the convention. More than 30 provisions mentioned in the Pinckney Draught were incorporated into the final Constitution. These provisions included eliminating religious testing as a qualification for holding public office, assigning impeachment power to the House of Representatives, and establishing a single chief executive. Disliked by James Madison—whose journals provide the best source of information about the convention— the pompous Pinckney never received the credit he deserved for his contributions. Since his personal papers were later destroyed by fire, no records survive today to tell Pinckney's side of the story.*

Cottage

The rectangular plan, side gable roof and wide front porch of this modest c.1828 home are all elements shared by 19C coastal cottages. Inside, there's no furniture, but informative panels describe Pinckney's life and his career as a statesman, which included three terms as South Carolina governor, one term in the US Senate, and a four-year stint as ambassador to Spain under President Thomas Jefferson.

Grounds

Follow the half-mile walking trail to discover the archaeological research underway on-site. To date, scientists have found the vestiges of a detached kitchen, a privy and a slave village. The latter reveals a wealth of information about the area's African-American heritage.

FORT MOULTRIE★

1214 Middle St., on Sullivans Island. 9mi northeast of Charleston via US-17 North and Rte. 703 - ☎843-883-3123 - www.nps.gov/fosu/historyculture/ fort_moultrie.htm - Open year-round daily 9am-5pm - Closed Jan 1, Thanksgiving Day and Dec 25 - $3 adults, $5 family pass (ages 15 and under free) - ♿.

Hastily built with wood from abundant local palmetto trees, the first fort on Sullivans Island was constructed in 1776 to protect Charleston from British attack. Soon afterward, Fort Moultrie gained fame as the crude rampart that held off the British during the battle for Sullivans Island. Soft palmetto logs that formed the walls of the early fort helped thwart the Redcoats' attack by absorbing the British shells. After the battle, the palmetto tree was adopted as the South Carolina state symbol. In 1794 Fort Moultrie was rebuilt as a five-sided battlement with earth and

Courtesy of the National Park Service

59

Fort Moultrie

timber walls, a structure which was destroyed by a hurricane in 1804. The third incarnation of the fort, the one you see here now, arose in 1809 and saw action through World War II. Fort Moultrie was decommissioned in 1947. Begin at the visitor center, where you'll find exhibits documenting the history of the fort. As you walk through the fort itself, you'll find remains from every period of its long history, including the site of the first fort; Cannon Walk, with its Civil War artillery; the two batteries that defended the harbor beginning in 1898; and a World War II Control Post. Outside the fort's Sally Port lie the graves of the Seminole leader Osceola, who died here in 1838, and

5 of the 62 crewmen who died when the US warship Patapsco was sunk in nearby waters in 1965.

BOONE HALL PLANTATION

1235 Long Point Rd., Mt. Pleasant. 8mi north of Charleston via US-17 North (Boone Hall is across from Charles Pinckney National Historic Site) - ☎843-884-4371 - www. boonehallplantation.com - Open Mar - Labor Day Mon-Sat 8:30am-6:30pm, Sun noon-5pm - Rest of the year Mon-Sat 9am–5pm, Sun noon-5pm - Closed Thanksgiving Day and Dec 25 - $24 adults, $12 children (ages 6-12) - Café. You'll feel like Scarlett O'Hara as you drive the three-quarter-mile avenue

Boone Hall Annual Events

- *Lowcountry Oyster Festival - Jan*
- *Strawberry Festival - Apr*
- *Scottish Games - Sept*
- *Boone Hall Pumpkin Patch - Oct*
- *Boone Hall Fright Nights - Oct*
- *Wine under the Oaks - Dec*
- *Boone Hall Plantation Christmas - Dec*

lined by centuries-old moss-draped live oaks leading to Boone Hall. Built in the 1700s, this former cotton plantation is named for Major John Boone, who acquired the 17,000 acres of land in 1681 from the Lord Proprietors of the Carolina colony. Today the remaining 738 acres host visitors and many public and private

events. The grounds are a popular film location as well.

Admission to Boone Hall includes a house tour and a 40-minute motor-coach tour of the grounds. It also gives you access to the **Butterfly Pavilion** *(open May-Sept)* and presentations relating to the local Gullah culture and the lives of the slaves who worked on the plantation (check schedules on-site).

Mansion

Visit by 30-minute guided tour only.
Constructed in 1935, the Colonial Revival-style main house respects the design of the original mid-18C structure, which was destroyed by fire. Guides in hoop skirts take you through the first-floor rooms, pointing out such treasures as the mahogany Hepplewhite dining room table and

60

Boone Hall Mansion

©Gwen Cannon/Michelin

©Brigitta L. House/Michelin

Oak-lined avenue leading to Boone Hall

the English Royal Crown Darby china trimmed in 24-karat gold.

Grounds

Located behind the Avenue of the Oaks, a group of unrestored slave cabins date back to 1743. The cabins, along with the smokehouse and cotton gin, were made with bricks produced on the plantation. The formal gardens contain varieties of antique roses dating back to the 16C.

Boone Hall Farms Market

2521 US-17, .5mi north of Long Point Rd. - ☎843-856-8154 - boone-hallfarms.com - Open year-round Mon-Sat 9am-7pm, Sun 10am-6pm (hours vary seasonally). About a mile from the plantation, this farm market does a brisk business in fresh local produce and preserved goods from Boone Hall. There's an on-site seafood market, a butcher shop, a florist shop and a cafe serving fresh lunch fare and homemade ice cream. Gourmet food items, wines and baked goods are also available for purchase.

CHARLES TOWNE LANDING STATE HISTORIC SITE

1500 Old Towne Rd., 3mi northwest of Charleston via US-17 to Rte. 171 - ☎843-852-4200 - southcarolinaparks.com - Open year-round daily 9am-5pm - Closed Dec 24 and 25 - $10 adults, $6 children (ages 6-15) - ♿.

Twist of Fate

*Known as the Merry Monarch, **King Charles II** returned from exile in 1661 to assume his throne. To reward those who had been most loyal to him, the King granted all the territory now occupied by North Carolina, South Carolina and Georgia to eight Lord Proprietors—aristocrats bearing titles of Duke, Earl or Sir, for the most part. In an interesting bit of historic irony, the Ashley and Cooper rivers in Charleston are named for one of the Lord Proprietors, Anthony Ashley Cooper, Earl of Shaftesbury, who was later imprisoned for plotting against his benefactor, King Charles.*

History comes alive at Charles Towne Landing, on the spot where the first English colonists landed in 1670. Here, they built a fort on Old Towne Creek and planted the fields with wheat, oranges, tobacco and other crops. Named Charles Towne, for King Charles II of England, the settlement lasted only 10 years in the swampy, mosquito-infested lands along the river. Plagued by disease and hunger, the colonists moved the town site across the river to the Charleston peninsula in 1680.

Experience early colonial life and the part African slaves played at the early settlement. As you explore the ruins of the first settlement, including a reconstruction of the original palisade wall, you'll see archaeology in action, as scientists are constantly unearthing the site's hidden past.

Visitor Center

Opened in 2006, the striking visitor center houses a gift shop and an interactive museum with exhibits on the voyage, the people and the settlement of Charles Towne. A digital dig showcases the archaeological process and on-site discoveries.

Trails and Gardens

Walk the self-guided history trail or rent a bike *($5/hr or $15/day)* and explore 7 miles of trails. Charles Towne's 80 acres of gardens include an Experimental Crop Garden showcasing crops—indigo, rice, sugarcane, cotton—the settlers tried to grow here.

Animal Forest

Bobcats and bison and wolves are just a few of the animals at this 22-acre zoo, in a natural forest setting. All the animals you'll find in this forest are the same types of critters that the first settlers found here.

The Adventure

Docked on Old Town Creek at Charles Towne Landing State Historic Site is *The Adventure*. A full-size replica of a 17C trading ship, this vessel is similar to the ships that would have carried goods in and out of Charleston Harbor during colonial days.

Legare-Waring House

The former home of philanthropist Ferdinanda Isabella Legare Backer Waring is open only as a special-events venue.

Charles Towne Landing State Historic Site

Hampton Park

Entrance on Cleveland St., off Rutledge Ave. - ☏843-724-7321 - www.charlestonparksconservancy.org. Just outside the Citadel's gates and bounded by Mary Murray Drive, Hampton Park embraces 60 acres of recreational space, including a large lake, a rose garden, a bandstand, and trails for walking, biking or jogging. Visitors enjoy the picnic tables, mature shade trees, well-equipped playground and ball fields too.

THE CITADEL

171 Moultrie St. - ☏843-225-3294 - www.citadel.edu - The campus is open to visitors year-round daily 8am-6pm. Rising northwest of the Historic District along the Ashley River, the white Moorish-style notched walls of the Citadel buildings surround green Summerall Field. This well-known military academy, which enrolls 3,400 men and women, began in 1829 as an arsenal and guardhouse to protect the city of Charleston. At that time, the Citadel was located on Marion Square (Calhoun and Meeting Sts.) in what is now downtown Charleston (the original building, now painted pink, remains on the square as an Embassy Suites hotel). In 1842 the Citadel, along with the Arsenal in Columbia, South Carolina, was converted into the South Carolina Military Academy. The academy remained on Marion Square until 1910, when it acquired the 200-acre campus on which it's now located.

Touring the Campus

Cadet-led tours of the campus are available during the school year *(to arrange a guided tour, call ☏843-953-5230)*. If you want to explore on your own, you can pick up a walking-tour brochure at the Citadel Museum in Daniel Library. You'll want to hit the major points of interest, including the Gothic-style **Summerall Chapel**, the **Mark Clark Grave**, burial place of Gen. Mark W. Clark, former president of the Citadel and one of the top American military commanders of World War II; and the 90-foot-high **Thomas Dry Howie Carillon Tower**, which rings out concerts with its 59 Dutch bells. Several monuments on the grounds honor the heroism of Citadel graduates.

Citadel Museum

Inside the Daniel Library, 3rd floor - ☏843-953-7535 - library.citadel.edu/museum - Open Mon-Fri 9am-5pm, Sun noon-5pm - Closed when classes are not in session. In this small museum, historic photos, uniforms, weapons, medals and other artifacts tell the story of the Citadel, from its founding in 1842 to its involvement in

Military Dress Parade

If you're into pomp and circumstance, visit on Friday afternoon at 3:45pm during the college year to see the cadets march across central Summerall Field in their crisp full-dress uniforms. Afterwards, you can stop by the Citadel gift shop and pick up a souvenir.

The End of a Journey

The eight-man crew who served aboard the Hunley were finally laid to rest on April 17, 2004. Ceremonies began in the morning with a poignant memorial service at White Point Gardens. After the service, a procession led by horse-drawn caissons traveled through the Historic District to Magnolia Cemetery on Charleston Neck (70 Cunningham Ave.), where 2,200 veterans of the Civil War are interred. Here, the crew of the Hunley was buried in front of a crowd of thousands of well-wishers, some of whom came from as far away as Australia.

If you're interested in visiting the cemetery at night, each October the Confederate Heritage Trust conducts its Ghost Walk by lantern light (not recommended for young children). For information and tickets, call ☎843-722-8638 or visit www. magnoliacemetery.net.

today's military operations around the world. Before you leave the library, note the Citadel Murals that illustrate the academy's history.

H. L. HUNLEY

1250 Supply St., on Charleston's former Naval Base. (from I-26, take Exit 216B/Cosgrove Ave. North) - ☎843-743-4865 - hunley.org - Visit by 30-minute guided tour only, year-round Sat 10am-5pm and Sun noon-5pm - Closed holiday weekends - $16 adults, $8 children (ages 6-7) - ♿. Off the coast of Charleston on the night of February 17, 1864, the Confederate submarine H.L. Hunley fired a 135-pound torpedo into the Union Navy warship USS *Housatonic*, commanded by Lt. George Dixon, successfully sinking it. The crew on this cylindrical iron boiler, held together with strips of iron and rivets, signaled to shore that they had completed their mission and were on their way back. Then, mysteriously, the sub disappeared.

In 1995, after being lost at sea for 131 years, the *Hunley* was found by adventurer Clive Cussler buried in the ocean floor just outside Charleston Harbor. The raising of the *Hunley*, a joint undertaking of the Department of the Navy, the Park Service, Oceaneering International Inc., and Friends of the Hunley, was a feat of oceanic proportions. From a platform composed of two massive suction piles (the type used for mooring deepwater oil rigs), engineers lowered a truss onto the sub and positioned nylon slings with inflated foam pillows underneath the craft. On August 8, 2000, a crane lifted the entire truss to the surface and the vessel was placed on a transport barge.

Today scientists in the **Warren Lasch Conservation Center** in North Charleston are unraveling the mysteries of the *Hunley* and its courageous crew. You can learn about the submarine's construction and view the sub in its conservation tank by taking one of the weekend tours.

Day Trips to the Beach

Grab your towel and sunscreen and head for the wide expanses of sand that line the coast north and south of Charleston. From residential Isle of Palms★ to tony Kiawah Island★★ (◐see p.69), Charleston's barrier-island beaches make a great excursion. Spend the day at one of the area's public beach parks, and you're sure to find fun in the sun that the whole family will enjoy.

▶**Tip:** All Charleston County parks have the same opening hours and fees: May-Labor Day daily 9am-8pm - Rest of the year, daily 10am-sunset - May-Labor Day $10/vehicle, $15 Sat and Sun - Rest of the year, fees vary.

FOLLY BEACH COUNTY PARK

12mi south of Charleston. 1010 West Ashley Ave., on the west end of Folly Island - ☎843-5762-9660 - www.ccprc.com.
The closest sands to Charleston, bohemian Folly Beach caters to hordes of locals and visitors. Rent an umbrella and some chairs and stake out your spot along the 2,500 feet of oceanfront. The park offers the same amenities as Beachwalker Park, as well as a snack bar and boogie-board rentals in case the kids forgot their own boards. In summer, lifeguards patrol a designated beach area.

Folly Beach County Park and pier

© John A Allen / age fotostock

Beach and pier, Isle of Palms **67**

Folly Beach Fishing Pier

101 E. Arctic Ave., Folly Beach - ☎843-762-9516 - www.ccprc.com - Open May-Sept 6am-11pm - Rest of the year hours vary - $5 adults, $3 children (ages 12 and under) - Pier parking $10 May-Labor Day Mon-Fri, $15 Sat & Sun (rest of year fees vary).

Extending 1,045ft out into the water, the nearby **Edwin S. Taylor Folly Beach Fishing Pier** invites avid anglers to drop a line and see what's biting. Rods can be rented at the pier (*$10 full-day plus $25 deposit*).

Surfing at Folly

The area known to local surfers as The Washout (the beach north of the pier along East Ashley Ave.) is famed for having the best waves on the South Carolina coast, due to

Beach Rentals

Beach chair and umbrella rentals are available at all county beaches:
- *Beach chair - $10/day*
- *Beach umbrella - $15/day*
- *2 chairs & 1 umbrella - $30/day*
- *After 4pm, 1 chair or 1 umbrella is*
- *$5/each.*

Folly or Folly?

The label Folly Beach originally came from the Old English word meaning "dense foliage," which is likely what the early settlers found along the coast here. Today, though, the tiny beach town with its carefree attitude identifies more with the modern definition of the word.

McKevlin's Surf Shop

*Entrance on Cleveland St., off 8 Center St. - ✆843-588-2247 - www.mckevlins.com - Open daily 10am-5:30pm (until 6pm in spring & summer). One of the oldest surf shops on the East Coast, McKevlin's was established in 1965 by local surfer Dennis McKevlin and his son Ted. Today the shop has 3,300 square feet of retail space filled with surfboards, bodyboards, T-shirts and car racks. For the latest on where the best waves are breaking, call **McKevlin's Surf Report** line: 843-588-2261.*

an unimpeded wind effect from the shore. For more information on prime surfing spots, check online at www.follybeach.com.

ISLE OF PALMS COUNTY PARK

12mi northeast of Charleston - 1–14th Aves., Isle of Palms - ✆843-762-9957 - www.ccprc.com.
Just a 30-minute drive north of downtown Charleston, the

six-mile-long Isle of Palms makes a great escape from the city's often-crowded urban streets. This is a real beach community, with a large year-round population. Besides lifeguards (in summer) and all the other amenities found at Folly Beach and Beachwalker Park, Isle of Palms County Park has a children's play area and a sand volleyball court. Directly behind the beach you'll find a recently spruced-up commercial strip

68

Kiawah Beachwalker County Park

Sea Turtle Season

Loggerhead sea turtles (Caretta caretta) nest along the coast of South Carolina each year from mid-May through October. Females will dig a nest in the sand, where they lay up to 150 ping-pong-ball-size eggs that will incubate for 54 to 60 days. After emerging from their eggs at night, the hatchlings instinctively move away from the shadows and seek the brightest horizon—normally the ocean. Glaring lights of beachfront development confuse the young turtles, who often head in the wrong direction, decreasing their chances of survival.

Loggerhead turtle

The **South Carolina Aquarium★★** *(Ⓛsee p 27) in partnership with the South Carolina Dept. of Natural Resources (SCDNR) sponsors a Sea Turtle Rescue Program to help this threatened species (all seven species of sea turtles are either endangered or threatened). When SCDNR finds a stranded or injured sea turtle, they bring it to the Sea Turtle Hospital at the aquarium for treatment. Rehabilitated sea turtles are released back into the ocean.*

Several areas, including Kiawah Island and Folly Beach, have organized groups that patrol the beaches and fence off the turtle nests so that beachgoers don't inadvertently destroy them. If you see signs of turtle activity, be sure not to disturb the nests.

69

featuring metered parking, shops, beachfront bars, and an outpost of Ben and Jerry's ice cream *(closed in winter)*. The pier here is not open to the public.

KIAWAH BEACHWALKER COUNTY PARK

8 Beachwalker Dr., 21mi south of Charleston on the west end of Kiawah Island - 📞*843-762-9964 - www.ccprc.com.*
If you want to experience the spectacular beach on **Kiawah Island★★** but don't want to rent

lodgings at the private resort, spend a day at Beachwalker Park. Located just outside the resort's gates, the county park offers equipment rentals, lifeguards (in summer), dressing areas, outdoor showers, bathrooms and picnic areas with grills.
For supplies, there's a convenience store and gas station right on Beachwalker Drive as you turn off Kiawah Island Parkway.

Overnight Coastal Excursions

You'll need to plan at least a couple of days to experience some of the resort destinations and white sands that line the coast from Myrtle Beach, South Carolina down to Georgia's Golden Isles. These places are all worth a visit in their own right while you're in the area.

▶**Tip:** It's best to have a car for these excursions, but if not, you can still reach these coastal destinations via public transportation (◉see p. 171).

THE GRAND STRAND★★

Fun is the order of the day on this 60-mile beachfront that marches up the coast of South Carolina along US-17 from Georgetown (60mi north of Charleston) to Little River. Sandwiched between the Intracoastal Waterway on the west and the Atlantic Ocean on the east, the Grand Strand's nerve center is **Myrtle Beach★**. To the south lie the low-key coastal communities of Surfside Beach, Murrells Inlet (great for fresh seafood), Litchfield Beach and Pawleys Island. In addition to the lure of the sand and surf, the area draws duffers from across the country to its 100-plus golf courses, many of them championship-level links.

BROOKGREEN GARDENS★★

1931 Brookgreen Dr., in Murrells Inlet (3mi south of Pawleys Island off US-17) - ℘843-235-6000 - www. brookgreen.org - Open year-round daily 9:30am-5pm (hours vary

Touring Tip

Admission tickets to Brookgreen include daily garden walks, tours and special programs. A shuttle regularly tranports visitors to the gardens, the Lowcountry Center and the zoo. Otherwise, walking is the mode of transport (no vehicles allowed). Guided walking tours of the Sculpture Garden are offered (11am, noon & 2pm). No pets are allowed in the gardens.

*The **Oaks Plantation History and Nature Trail** is an additional $8 ($4 for children). Tickets for access and walking tours are available at the Lowcountry Center. A mini-bus transports visitors to the remote plantation location Mar-Nov Mon & Wed at 11am & 1pm.*

seasonally) - Closed Dec 25 - $16 adults, $8 children (ages 4-12) - Restaurant - Café.
Art and nature combine to form a stunning landscaped setting here. Opened in 1932 as America's first sculpture garden, Brookgreen is

©Gwen Cannon/Michelin

Anna Hyatt Huntington's sculpture at entrance of Brookgreen Gardens

the love-child of artist **Anna Hyatt Huntington** and her husband, Archer, who created the gardens on the 900-acre grounds of an antebellum rice plantation. The property features several attractions that are especially enticing to younger visitors: the **Enchanted Storybook Forest**, an assortment of small-scale playhouses based on classic stories and nursery rhymes; and the **Butterfly House** *(open Apr-Nov - $3 adults, $2 children ages 4-12)*; and the on-site **Lowcountry Zoo**.

Huntington Sculpture Garden

This 30-acre display garden forms Brookgreen's centerpiece. Here, major sculptures anchor individual garden rooms, serving as focal points at the end of long walkways. The noted sculpture collection, most of which is displayed outside in the gardens, contains more than 800 works of **American sculpture** (early 19C to present) by renowned sculptors such as Daniel Chester French, Augustus St. Gaudens, Paul Manship, and Anna Hyatt Huntington herself.

Lowcountry Zoo

In a wooded expanse opposite the gardens, the Carolina coast's only zoo accredited by the Association of Zoos and Aquariums shelters bald eagles, river otters, red foxes, white-tailed deer and other native critters. Many of these animals found a home

Creek Cruises

Cruises (1hr) depart from the dock at the Lowcountry Center Mar-Nov daily 11am, noon, 2pm & 3pm - $8 adults, $4 children (ages 12 & under) - Evening cruises may be available in summer (bring mosquito repellant) - Buying tickets upon arrival is advised, as cruises often sell out. Kids and adults alike will enjoy a ride on Brookgreen's 48-foot-long pontoon boat, which travels deep inside the preserve through blackwater creeks once tapped to irrigate rice fields. Now, instead of rice paddies, the wetlands are home to alligators, snakes, hawks, osprey, and a host of other creatures. Along the way, your guide will tell you about the labors involved in cultivating and harvesting the rice known as Carolina Gold (☙ see p. 55).

72

at Brookgreen because they were injured and unable to live on their own in the wild. A cypress swamp is inhabited by alligators, and along the boardwalk in the Cypress Aviary, visitors might spot egrets, wooded mergansers and black-crowned night herons, among other species. At **River Basin Retreat**, an 8,000 gallon above-ground pool serves as a playground for the resident otters. Domestic plantation animals such as Red Devon cattle, Marsh Tacky horses and Tunis sheep are also on view. These heritage breeds are more characteristic of animals in the 1800s than of their hybrid counterparts of today. For a closer look at the area's fauna, take one of the creek cruises.

HUNTINGTON BEACH STATE PARK ★

16148 Ocean Hwy., Murrells Inlet, across from Brookgreen Gardens on east side of US-17 - ☎843-237-4440 - southcarolinaparks.com - Open year-round daily 6am-6pm (until 10pm during Daylight Saving Time) -

$5 adults, $3 children (ages 6-15). The Nature Center is currently closed, as it is being rebuilt following a fire. Want an escape from the crowds and development at Myrtle Beach? Huntington Beach is the place. This glorious state park boasts three miles of undeveloped beachfront where nothing towers higher than the sea oats. Acres of pristine salt marshes (follow the boardwalk) draw devoted birdwatchers hoping to spot any of the more than 300 species of birds. The marshes are considered among the best birdwatching sites in the southeastern US.

The park is home to **Atalaya**, once the winter residence of Anna Hyatt and Archer Huntington, who founded nearby Brookgreen Gardens (☙ *p. 70*). You can tour the Moorish-style castle *(open daily 9am-4pm, until 5pm during Daylight Saving Time - $2 - floorplan available with admission fee).* There's camping in the park, and nature lovers can discover the diverse wildlife of the site's marshland ecosystem on their own along the trails and boardwalks

©NDJordan/Michelin

Atalaya, Huntington Beach State Park

extending out into the marshes, or via the various land and water field trips offered through the Coastal Exploration Program *(Mar-Nov)*.

MYRTLE BEACH★

98mi north of Charleston on US-17 - Visitor information: ☏843-626-7444 or ☏800-356-3016 - www. visitmyrtlebeach.com - Visitor center at 1200 N. Oak St. and a welcome center at the airport.

The pulsing playground that is Myrtle Beach booms nearly year-round with people, traffic and entertainment options. Before 1900, however, this part of the coast was a quiet backwater. Enter the Burroughs and Collins Company, a turpentine manufacturer who built the first hotel on the beach in 1901. The wife of the company's founder named the area Myrtle Beach, for the abundance of wax myrtle trees that grew wild along the shore. After Hurricane Hazel razed the Grand Strand in 1954, the ensuing rebuilding boom incorporated golf courses into the mix of hotels, restaurants, and the plethora of entertainment that includes amusement parks, mini-golf, concert venues and family-friendly dinner shows. In the 1970s and 80s and on into the 21C, residential and commercial projects mushroomed, resulting in the mega-resort you see here today.

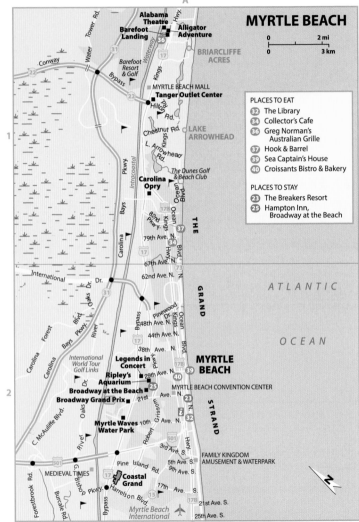

MYRTLE BEACH

0 — 2 mi
0 — 3 km

BRIARCLIFFE ACRES

Alabama Theatre
Barefoot Landing
Alligator Adventure

Barefoot Resort & Golf

MYRTLE BEACH MALL
Tanger Outlet Center

LAKE ARROWHEAD

The Dunes Golf & Beach Club
Carolina Opry

THE

82nd Ave. N.
79th Ave. N.
67th Ave. N.
62nd Ave. N.

ATLANTIC

GRAND

48th Ave. N.
44th Ave. N.
38th Ave. N.

OCEAN

International World Tour Golf Links
Legends in Concert
Ripley's Aquarium
Broadway at the Beach
Broadway Grand Prix

MYRTLE BEACH

MYRTLE BEACH CONVENTION CENTER

Myrtle Waves Water Park

STRAND

FAMILY KINGDOM AMUSEMENT & WATERPARK

MEDIEVAL TIMES
Coastal Grand

Myrtle Beach International

THE MARKET COMMON   MYRTLE BEACH STATE PARK

74

PLACES TO EAT
- **32** The Library
- **34** Collector's Cafe
- **36** Greg Norman's Australian Grille
- **37** Hook & Barrel
- **39** Sea Captain's House
- **40** Croissants Bistro & Bakery

PLACES TO STAY
- **23** The Breakers Resort
- **25** Hampton Inn, Broadway at the Beach

Myrtle Beach Entertainment

With all the attractions at Myrtle Beach, it's nearly impossible to be bored. Here are some options for things to do.

Alabama Theatre – *4750 US-17 S, at Barefoot Landing, North Myrtle Beach - ☎843-272-1111 - www.alabama-theatre.com.* This theater presents a regular schedule of comedy and music shows featuring guest artists like Alabama, Vince Gill, and the Four Tops, in addition to its signature musical and dance extravaganza, ONE, The Show.

Alligator Adventure – *4604 US-17, at Barefoot Landing, North Myrtle Beach - ☎843-361-0789 - alligatoradventure. com - Check online for details of free second-day pass.* If you haven't come across any alligators in your Lowcountry wanderings, you're sure to see some here, along with snakes, tortoises, ring-tailed lemurs and tropical birds as you explore the marshes and swamps.

Broadway Grand Prix – *1820 21st Ave. N. Ext., US-17 Bypass and 21st Ave. N. Ext. - ☎843-839-4080 - broadwaygrandprix.com.* This 26-acre amusement park—once the official property of the National Association for Stock Car Auto Racing—has seven go-kart racetracks ranging from the Grand Prix Pro (riders must be 60" or taller) to tamer tracks for all skill levels and ages.

Carolina Opry – *8901 N. Kings Highway at US-17 Bypass - ☎843-913-4000 or ☎800-843-6779 - www. thecarolinaopry.com.* Now in its 32nd season, the Carolina Opry presents

© NDJordan/Michelin

Looking north along the coast, Myrtle Beach

Carolina Safari Jeep Tours

Departures usually leave the parking lot of the Carolina Opry (8901 N. Kings Hwy.) - Open year-round Mon-Sat 9:15am, Sun 10am (phone reservations required) - ☎843-497-5337 - carolinasafari.com - $48 adults, $44 teens, $38 children (ages 4-12). Climb aboard these covered custom Jeeps for a look at the wilder side of Myrtle Beach—the naturally wild side, that is. On the 3-1/2-hour excursion, you'll explore a Waccamaw Neck oyster bed, a barrier island, and several historic sites, including the churchyard where American poet James Dickey lies buried.

music, dance and comedy in live shows inside the 2,200-seat Calvin Gilmore Theater.

Legends in Concert – *2925 Hollywood Dr., Myrtle Beach (Hwy. 17 bypass at 29th Ave. N.)* – *☎843-238-7827 - www.legendsinconcert.com*. Elvis may not be here anymore, but you can see his like belt out The King's greatest hits in this celebrity tribute show at Broadway at the Beach. The changing lineup of performers could include Cher, Tim MCGraw and Bruno Mars.

Myrtle Waves Water Park – *3000 10th Ave. N. Ext US-17 Bypass and 10th Ave. N.* - *☎843-913-9250 - www.myrtlewaves.com*. Beat the summer heat at this 20-acre water park, where you can tube along a lazy river and play in the surf at the Ocean in Motion wave pool. Rocket down the dark Turbo Twister tube slides, and experience the high-intensity thrill of the Rockin' Ray tube slide. The 23 water rides and attractions include the tamer Bubble Bay for toddlers.

Pavilion Park – *1171 Celebrity Circle., at Broadway at the Beach (US-17 Bypass and 29th Ave. N.)* - *☎843-839-0303 - pavilion-park.com*. Harking back to the past with arcade games and cotton candy, this family-friendly amusement park is divided into three parks: east, west and central. East offers old-time attractions like a 1905 Herschell-Spillman carousel. West adds a Ferris wheel and the new Myrtle Turtle Coaster, while Central boasts thrill rides.

Ripley's Aquarium – *1110 Celebrity Circle, at Broadway at the Beach* - *☎843-916-0888 - www.ripleysaquarium.com – Ask about combination tickets*. Travel on the moving glidepath through the **Dangerous Reef,** where you'll be completely surrounded by 750,000 gallons of salt water and sea creatures from sharks to sea turtles. Stick around for the dive and feeding shows (ask at admission desk for a schedule of events).

Myrtle Beach Golf

Some 4 million rounds of golf are played in the Myrtle Beach area each year on local courses. While the courses are way too numerous to list them all here, the following are among the top rated courses. For a complete list of courses, check online at: www.myrtlebeachgolf.com or www.mbn.com.

Barefoot Resort and Golf – *4980 Barefoot Resort Bridge Rd., North Myrtle Beach -* 📞*866-638-4818 - barefootgolf.com.* Choose among the four courses here according to your favorite designer: Tom Fazio, Pete Dye, Davis Love III or Greg Norman.

Caledonia Golf and Fish Club – *369 Caledonia Dr., Pawleys Island -* 📞*843-237-3675 - www.fishclub.com.* Caledonia is consistently rated among the country's top public courses in the golf press.

The Dunes Golf and Beach Club – *9000 N. Ocean Blvd., Myrtle Beach -* 📞*843-449-5236 - www.thedunes club.net.* This Robert Trent Jones course is private, but tee times are available for guests of partner hotels.

Myrtle Beach Mini Golf

Sure, you'll get your time on the links, but what about the kids? With 50 mini-golf courses in the Myrtle Beach area, you'll be hard-pressed to avoid them, no matter where you go. Choose a theme, from prehistoric dinosaurs to pirate ships to erupting volcanoes. For a list of area courses, check online at www.golflink.com/miniature-golf.

Tidewater Golf Club – *1400 Tidewater Dr., North Myrtle Beach -* 📞*843-466-8754 - www.tidewatergolf.com.* Often compared to the famed Pebble Beach Links, Tidewater sits high on a bluff surrounded by the Intracoastal Waterway, salt marsh and ocean.

Broadway at the Beach

Myrtle Beach Shopping

Don't wait for a rainy day to check out the myriad shopping malls and more than 300 outlet stores in Myrtle Beach. Most stores open at 10am; closing hours vary by season.

Barefoot Landing – *4898 US-17 S., North Myrtle Beach (adjacent to Barefoot Resort)* - ☏843-272-8349 - *www.bflanding.com.* Set around a 27-acre lake, Barefoot Landing encompasses 100 specialty shops, and several factory outlets in addition to its other attractions.

Broadway at the Beach – *US-17 Bypass at 21st Ave. N.* - ☏843-444-3200 - *www.broadwayatthebeach. com.* This lakeside complex embraces hotels, nightclubs, movie theaters, and attractions. You'll also find 100 retail and outlet stores.

Coastal Grand Mall – *2000 Coastal Grand Circle, US-17 Bypass at Hwy. 501* - ☏843-839-9100 - *www.coastalgrand.com.* The area's biggest enclosed mall has Southern-region department-store anchors Belk and Dillard's, plus 100 other national brand retailers.

The Market Common – *4017 Deville St., Farrow Pkwy.* - ☏843-839-3500 - *www.marketcommonmb.com.* On 114 acres of a former Air Force base, this upscale oasis includes retail, residential, recreational, dining and retail space.

Tanger Outlet Centers – *10835 Kings Rd., Myrtle Beach (US-17 at Hwy. 22)* - ☏843-449-0491 - *www.tangeroutlet. com.* Between its two locations (the second at 4635 Factory Stores Blvd.,

on Hwy.501), Tanger offers some 175 outlet stores stocking everything from designer clothes to cookware.

MYRTLE BEACH STATE PARK★

401 S. Kings Hwy., 4mi south of Myrtle Beach on US Business 17 - ☏843-238-5325 - *southcarolinaparks.com. Open Mar-Nov daily 6am-10pm - Rest of year daily 6am-8pm - $5 adults, $3 children (ages 6-15).*
Pining for a beach without the backdrop of high-rise hotels? Head for this quiet 312-acre state park. Developed by the Civilian Conservation Corps in the 1930s, it preserves a one-mile stretch of beachfront and one of the last stands of maritime forest on this part of the South Carolina coast. The park is also a great spot for surf-fishing.

HAMPTON PLANTATION STATE HISTORIC SITE

1950 Rutledge Rd., MCClellanville. 16mi southwest of Georgetown off US-17 - ☏843-546-9361 - *southcarolinaparks.com - Grounds open year-round daily 9am-5pm (6pm Apr-Oct) - House visit by 1hr guided tour only, year-round Mon, Tue and Fri noon and 2pm. Sat-Sun 10am, noon and 2pm - $7.50 adults, $3.50 children (ages 6-15) - Closed Thanksgiving Day and Dec 25.*
A French Huguenot family by the name of Horry established this rice plantation in the mid-18C. Today the 274-acre Lowcountry estate showcases the white Georgian-style mansion that began as a six-room

The Original Indigo Girl

Born to a British Army officer stationed in Antigua, Eliza Lucas (1722–1793) was 16 when her father, Lt. Col. George Lucas, moved the family to a plantation in South Carolina. The same year, Lucas was recalled to his post in Antigua, leaving his teenage daughter to run the plantation. After her father sent her some indigo seeds from the West Indies, the young girl spent three years cultivating the plant and learning to extract the deep-blue dye—in great demand in England for military uniforms. Thanks to Eliza's successful experiments, Charleston's export of indigo mushroomed from 5,000 pounds in 1746 to 130,000 pounds two years later.

In 1744 Eliza married widower Charles Pinckney and assumed the management of several of her husband's estates. Their sons, Charles Cotesworth (🕑see p. 58) and Thomas, both distinguished themselves in early American politics. When she died in 1793, Eliza Lucas Pinckney was so revered that President George Washington, who had visited the plantation in 1791, insisted on being a pallbearer at her funeral.

farmhouse in 1750. Its columned two-story portico was added in 1791 by Daniel Huger Horry. Horry's mother-in-law, **Eliza Lucas Pinckney**, brought the design back from England. The last of the family line to occupy the residence was Archibald Rutledge, Poet Laureate of South Carolina, who died here in 1973. Unfurnished, the house is unrestored in places in order to illustrate the original building techniques, such as the timber framing with its mortise-and-tenon joints, used to construct the house. The remnants of rice fields can be seen at Wambaw Creek.

HOPSEWEE PLANTATION

494 Hopsewee Rd., Georgetown, 30mi south of Brookgreen Gardens off US-17 - ☎843-546-7891 - hopsewee. com - Visit by 1hr guided tour only, Feb-late Dec Tue-Sat 10am-3pm

- Closed January and major holidays - $20 adults, $10.50 youth (ages 12–17), $7.50 children (ages 5–11) - Grounds only, $7.50/person - Café.
Set on the Santee River, this Lowcountry indigo plantation is remarkable as the birthplace of Thomas Lynch Jr., who at age 26 was the youngest legislator to sign the Declaration of Independence. Lynch and his father, Thomas Sr., were the only father-and-son pair to serve as members of the nation's Continental Congress.

Made of black cypress, the two-story Georgian home (1740), with its steep hipped roof and graceful double piazza (added in 1846), is now privately owned. Inside, you'll see fine examples of 18C and 19C American and European furnishings. If you want to extend your visit, the on-site River Oak Cottage Tea Room serves a full lunch menu *(Tue-Sat 10:am-3:30pm)*.

Traveling for Health?

In 1776 the junior Thomas Lynch retired from political life due to health problems. After living at nearby Peachtree Plantation for three years, Lynch and his wife, Elizabeth, decided to take a trip to Europe, hoping that a change of climate would improve his failing health. In a cruel twist of fate, their ship was lost at sea on the outgoing voyage. None of the passengers survived.

PAWLEYS ISLAND

24 miles south of Myrtle Beach along US-17.

Colonial rice planters had the right idea. They began coming to Pawleys Island in the 19C to escape their mosquito-infested plantations. Today shabby-chic Pawleys Island and its swankier next-door neighbor, Litchfield Beach, cater to visitors who rent houses and condos along this four-mile stretch of sand on the east side of the Waccamaw River. An island-wide ban on Myrtle Beach-style commercial and industrial development renders Pawleys peaceful, laid-back and relaxed, with crabbing, birdwatching and fishing as the activities of choice. You won't find blaring radios, beach volleyball, noisy jet skis here—just quiet sunning, swimming and strolling.

Although Pawleys Island claims some of the prettiest beaches on the Grand Strand, it's difficult to access them if you're not staying on the island. Most of the land is private, with few public beach-access points.

Hammock Shops Village

10880 Ocean Hwy. (US-17), Pawleys Island - www.thehammockshops. com. Fronting nearly two dozen stores and eateries, all connected by paths winding beneath tall pines, the **Original Hammock Shop** (*&843-237-9122 - hammockshop. com*)—a Pawleys Island staple since the 1930s—occupies a Lowcountry-style cottage. This is the home of the world-famous Pawleys Island rope hammocks. Attached to it, the General Store stocks beach clothes,

The Humble Hammock

What do you do when the grass-filled mattresses on your riverboat prove too hot and uncomfortable during the humid summers in the Lowcountry? You invent a rope bed. At least, that's what Captain Joshua John Ward did in the late 1800s. Ward, who transported supplies to the large rice plantations around Georgetown, South Carolina, came up with the idea of making a hanging bed of rope, to allow for greater air circulation. And it was portable, to boot.

For more than 100 years, his invention has remained unaltered. It still serves as the design for the Pawleys Island hammocks sold at the Original Hammock Shop today. Take one home for those alfresco naps.

books, birdhouses—but is known for its fudge, which comes in a variety of flavors. In the adjacent **Hammock Weaver's Pavilion**, artisans craft Pawleys Island's rope hammocks. Popular stores Affordables and Pawleys Island Wear specialize in casual women's attire, and Island Shoes carries must-have handbags and women's footwear, and The Freckled Frog offers a wonderland of children's toys, books and games.

LOWCOUNTRY COAST★

Named for the soggy coastal prairies that line the low-lying South Carolina coast north and south of Charleston, the Lowcountry incorporates quaint towns and a unique geography marked by vast expanses of water-laced marshes. Here you'll discover a host of wildlife along with a range of attractions from Gullah heritage sites to the upscale resort islands of Isle of Palms, Kiawah and Hilton Head. Whether it's peace and quiet or action you seek, you'll find it along the Lowcountry Coast.

KIAWAH ISLAND★★

21mi south of Charleston via the James Island Expressway and Maybank Hwy. (Rte. 700) - ✆843 -768-2121 or ✆800-654-2924 - www.kiawahresort.com.
Named for the Indians who hunted and fished here for hundreds of years before the first Europeans arrived,

© D. Duncan/ Getty Images

Kiawah Island wildlife

Wildlife, Wildlife, Everywhere

You'll share Kiawah's semi-tropical paradise with a host of critters. Flocks of egrets, great blue herons, ospreys and other water birds feed in the marshes in the early morning and at dusk. Plan a walk or a bike ride, and don't forget your binoculars. You may see deer on the island at any time of day—but especially after dusk—so be sure to heed posted speed limits.

You'll also spy some good-size alligators sunning themselves on the banks of Kiawah's many waterways. They normally keep to themselves, as long as you don't bother them. Never, ever, feed an alligator! They become dangerous once they start associating humans with food. The reptiles' small brains don't distinguish between the food in your hand and your hand itself. They may look sluggish, but alligators can sprint at speeds nearing 15mph for distances of 50 yards—that's faster han you can run.

Kiawah Island embraces 10,000 breathtaking acres of maritime forest and pristine tidal marsh. In the 18C, the island was first owned by Revolutionary War hero General Arnoldus Vanderhorst, who raised Sea Island cotton here. After the Civil War, the land saw a succession of different owners until 1974, when it was developed as a resort and residential community. Today Kiawah's 10 miles of uninterrupted white beach provide plenty of space for relaxation.

Bohicket Marina

Just off Kiawah Island and right outside the gates to private Seabrook Island, Bohicket Marina's location facing west on Haulover Creek makes it a great place to watch the sunset. While you're there, you can also browse the shops, have a bite in one of the Market's eateries, take a cruise, schedule a fishing expedition or rent a boat.

The Sanctuary is a luxurious oceanfront hotel and spa that opened in 2004 to round out the offerings of this world-class resort.

Resort Activities

If you're tired of sunbathing, try championship golf and tennis or bike the 30 miles of trails around the island (rent bikes at Night Heron Park and The Sanctuary). Take the kids to the playground or the fun-filled children's pool at 21-acre Night Heron Park, which boasts two flume slides and a toddler splash zone. In case you consider eating to be a sport, there are 11 eateries to choose from on the resort grounds.

Golf – Kiawah's five scenic golf courses, which include the world-renowned **Ocean Course**, were designed by some of the biggest names in golf.

Tennis – Two tennis complexes on the property include 19 clay courts and 5 hard courts. There's even a

© Alan Tobey/iStockphoto.com

Historic home in Beaufort

practice court with a machine that will retrieve your balls for you. Tennis pro Roy Barth, a member of the Southern Tennis Hall of Fame, has been on staff here since 1976.

Kiawah's Nature Program hosts naturalist-led canoe trips, sea-kayaking excursions and bird walks.

Kamp Kiawah – *843-768-6001 - www.kiawahresort.com*. Don't feel guilty about dropping the kids off at Kamp Kiawah. Youngsters ages 3 to 7 will stay entertained here with the likes of pirate adventures, crabbing, sand sculpting, swimming and crafts, while older kids age 8-15 will find thrills at **Camp Xtreme**. And it's all supervised fun (rates vary by season and program; reservations required).

BEAUFORT★

70mi south of Charleston via US-17 to US-21 South - Visitor information: 843-525-8500 - www.beaufortsc.org.
If Beaufort looks familiar to you, it's probably because the town has starred as the backdrop in so many movies—*The Big Chill, Forrest Gump, The Prince of Tides* and *Rules of Engagement*, to name a few. The town's palmetto-lined streets, elegant architecture, moss-draped live oaks and flat tidal marshes make it the quintessential Southern setting. Make your first stop the **Visitor Center** for a brief introduction to the town. **Bay Street**, Beaufort's main street, runs along the water and is

84

Touring Tip

In Beaufort, leave your car at **Waterfront Park** *(Bay & Newcastle Sts.), where a marina edges the Beaufort River. Bordering the park, Bay Street teems with shops, restaurants, and historic houses, most of which are privately owned. Walking-tour brochures are available at the* **Beaufort Visitors Center** *(713 Craven St. in the 1798 Arsenal - open year-round Mon-Sat 9am-5pm - closed Sun & holidays).*

lined with shops and eateries. Nearby, at **Blackstone's Cafe** *(205 Scott St.; ☎843-524-4330; blackstonescafe.com)*, you can start your day with a shrimp omelette. The walkable 304-acre **historic district** takes in the entire original town of Beaufort (pronounced BYEW-furt), chartered as part of Britain's Carolina colony in 1711. Spend a leisurely day here to get an intimate look at the wealth generated by South Carolina's 18C and 19C planter class. The city's waterfront park spreads out along the Beaufort River.

On Wednesdays *(May-Oct 2pm-6pm)*, a **farmer's market** stretches from West Street to Craven Street.

John Verdier House Museum

801 Bay St. - ☎843-379-6335 - www.historicbeaufort.org - Visit by 30-minute guided tour only, year-round Mon-Sat 10:30am-3:30pm on the half-hour - Closed Sun and major holidays - $10. In 1825, the Marquis de Lafayette slept in this early 19C Federal-style house, the only planter's house in Beaufort that is open to the public. Merchant John Verdier's residence illustrates the Beaufort style—with its raised first floor, double piazza, T-shaped floor plan, and shallow, hipped roof—designed to take full advantage of prevailing river breezes.

HILTON HEAD ISLAND ★

30mi south of Beaufort via I-95 South to US-278 East. Hilton Head/Bluffton Chamber of Commerce, 1 Chamber of Commerce Dr., Hilton Head - ☎843-785-3673 - www.hiltonheadisland.org.

Spanish Moss

You see it everywhere in the Lowcountry, hanging like fringe over the branches of live oak and cypress trees. A symbol of the South, Spanish moss is quite the misnomer: it's neither Spanish, nor moss. It is, in fact, an epiphyte, or air plant, which wraps its long silvery-green stems around a host tree and drapes from the tree's branches. The plant's narrow leaves are covered with scales that trap moisture and nutrients from the air. In the 18C, Spanish moss was used in many Southern households to stuff mattresses. The insects that were often trapped in this natural filler became known as bed bugs, as in "don't let the bed bugs bite."

HILTON HEAD ISLAND

CHARLESTON, BLUFFTON

Port Royal Sound

Pinckney Island

National Wildlife

Refuge

Hilton Head

Buckingham Landing

Brighton Beach

Jess Island

Palmetto Hall Plantation

Palmetto Hall Plantation

Plantation

Windmill Harbour

Welcome Center

Port Royal

Hilton Head Plantation

Spanish Wells Rd.

Spanish Wells Plantation

Pope Rd.

Skull Cr.

Seabrook Dr.

Mackay's

May River

Bull Creek

Barataria Island

Cross

Broad Creek

Sound

Indigo Run Golden Bear Golf Club

Mathews Dr.

Long Cove Plantation

Wexford Plantation

Marshland Rd.

William Hilton Pkwy.

Beach City Rd.

Folly Field Beach Park

Driessen Beach Pk.

Burkes Beach

Palmetto Dunes

Palmetto Dunes

ATLANTIC OCEAN

Palmetto Bay Rd.

Harbour Town Lighthouse

Harbour Town

Harbour Town Links

Sea Pines Resort

Plantation Dr.

Greenwood Dr.

Shipyard Plantation

Cordillo Pkwy.

Forest

Beach Dr.

Forest Beach

Coligny Beach Park

HILTON HEAD ISLAND ★

Daufuskie Island

Calibogue Sound

S. Sea Pines Dr.

Braddock Point

N

PLACES TO EAT
- Michael Anthony's Cucina Italiana
- Old Oyster Factory
- Red Fish

85

With its resorts, golf courses and tennis courts hidden amid 42 square miles of natural marshland and 12 miles of beach, Hilton Head ranks as one of South Carolina's most popular vacation destinations. Three tennis academies and The Golf Learning Center at Sea Pines Resort help make it a year-round magnet sports lovers. The island's namesake is English explorer William Hilton, who sailed into Calibogue Sound in 1663 and claimed the island for the British Crown. By 1860 two dozen plantations, growing cotton, indigo, sugar cane and rice, dotted the island. Development began almost a century later, when the two bridges connecting the island to the mainland opened in the mid-1950s. Today Hilton Head's 11 planned residential communities, many named for the antebellum plantations that once occupied their sites, take up half the island.

Touring Tip

Most of the commercial amenities on Hilton Head Island are located along William Hilton Parkway (US-278). It runs 11 miles from the northern end of the island down to Sea Pines Circle. Note that addresses on the island can be difficult to find, given the strict ordinances that prohibit neon signs and limit the height of commercial buildings.

Resorts

Here's a run-down of the island's resort communities that welcome vacationers:

Hilton Head Plantation – *7 Surrey Lane - www.hiltonheadplantation.com.* On the northern tip of the island, this 4,000-acre community has a beach on Calibogue Sound, four 18-hole golf courses and a large marina.

Palmetto Dunes – *4 Queens Folly Rd. - www.palmettodunes.com.* Here you can choose to rent a house or villa, or stay in one of two recently renovated resorts, the Hilton Head Marriott Resort and Spa and the Omni Hilton Head Island Oceanfront Resort. Palmetto Dunes' three golf courses are all open to the public.

Port Royal Plantation – *10A Coggins Point Rd. - www.portroyalplantation. net.* A lovely beach borders Port Royal, which incorporates the site of the original Hilton Head bluff. Houses here are not available for rent, but you can book a room at the Westin Hilton Head Island Resort and Spa.

Daufuskie Island

Once known for its Sea Island cotton and the oysters harvested offshore, eight-square-mile Daufuskie Island provides a quiet respite from Charleston and Hilton Head. Daufuskie's name comes from the Muscogee language, meaning "sharp feather," a reference to the island's shape. Visitors can tour the historic district (contact Tour Daufuskie - ☎843-842-9449 - tourdaufuskie.com) to learn the island's rich history, which includes a Gullah community—descendants of slaves left behind after the plantations closed—that peaked here in the 1940s.

Daufuskie's beach beckons with its soft sands and gentle surf. If you wish to stay overnight, cottages and villas are available to rent, and the island has a marina, several restaurants and a general store. Two public 18-hole golf courses offer Atlantic views. Bloody Point links (www.bloodypointresort.com) is named for a notorious 18C battle fought here between Native Americans and the British.

No cars are permitted on Daufuskie Island, but golf carts and bicycles can be rented - ☎843-757-9889 - www.daufuskieisland.com - Ferries depart twice a day from Buckingham Landing - 35 Fording Island Rd. Ext. (take US-278 over the Hilton Head Bridge) - ☎843-940-7704 - www.daufuskieislanferry.com - $35 round-trip.

Sea Pines Resort – *32 Greenwood Dr. - www.seapines.com.* Located on the south end of the island, Sea Pines is the first (1957) and the largest (5,200 acres) of Hilton Head's residential communities. Amenities include Harbour Town village, five miles of beach, two hotels and four golf courses (three of them public).

Shipyard Plantation – *10 Shipyard Dr. - shipyardhhi.com.* This 834-acre plantation includes the Shipyard Golf Club, the Sonesta Resort Hilton Head Island, and the Van der Meer Shipyard Tennis Resort.

Hilton Head Golf

Hilton Head has more than two dozen golf courses, 18 of which are open to the public. All of Hilton Head's courses are either located within, or associated with, one of the planned communities. Resort greens fees are on the expensive side, but vary depending on the course, the season, the day of the week, and the time of day you play. You'll often get the best deals in off-season (late Nov-Feb). For a complete list of courses, go online to: www.golfhiltonheadisland.net.

Harbour Town Lighthouse

149 Lighthouse Rd. - ☎ 843-671-2810 - $4.25 (free for kids age 5 and under)- www. harbourtownlighthouse.com - open daily 10am-6pm (closing times vary seasonally). A Hilton Head landmark, the hexagonal, red-and-white-striped lighthouse marks the northern point of Harbour Town's yacht basin. The working light is not operated by the government; it was built in 1970 by the developers of Sea Pines. Towering 93 feet above Calibogue Sound, the light serves as a beacon for local sailors and fishermen. Climb the 110 steps up to the observation deck for a sweeping view of the island.

© Richard Ellis / age fotostock

Harbour Town Lighthouse

Shelling on the Coast

Despite the fact that Blackbeard once prowled South Carolina's shore, the buried treasure you're most likely to find on these beaches is of the mollusk variety. Hunting for seashells can provide hours of fun for all members of the family. The wealth of seashells you might uncover at low tide—the best time to hunt for shells—includes fuzzy gray sand dollars, striped lightning whelks, snail-like baby's ears, colorful calico scallops, slender augers, and Atlantic clams.

Remember one rule of thumb: Never take shells with live creatures in them; you don't want to disturb some critter's home!

©NDJordan/Michelin

Golden Bear Golf Club – *72 Golden Bear Way* - ℘843-689-2200 - *www. clubcorp.com.* This semi-private course at Indigo Run is named for its designer, Jack Nicklaus, the Golden Bear.

Harbour Town Golf Links Course – *11 Lighthouse Lane, Sea Pines* - ℘843-363-8385 - *www.seapines.com.*

The renowned Pete Dye-designed course hosts the PGA's RBC Heritage tournament each year in April.

Palmetto Dunes – *4 Queens Folly Rd.* - ℘800-514-0085 - *www.palmetto dunes.com.* Choose among the wooded Arthur Hills Course, the lagoon-laden Robert Trent Jones Oceanfront Course, and par-70 George Fazio Course.

The Language That Time Forgot

*Yuh duh talk en Gullah? (Do you speak Gullah?) On the sea islands of South Carolina and Georgia, they do. These islands are home to a small community of African Americans who speak **Gullah**, remnants of a language passed on from the early slaves who worked the plantations on the mainland. Kidnapped from their homelands and unable to communicate with whites or with each other, the slaves created a unique language based on their different West African tongues. Also referred to as Geechee, this Creole dialect incorporates the West African languages of Vai, Mende, Twi and Ewe with words from English, Spanish and Dutch, among others. Gullah strongholds remain on St. Helena, Daufuskie Island (off the southern tip of Hilton Head) and Sapelo Island (Georgia State Parks offers tours of Sapelo Island - for information, call 912-437-3224 or check online at gastateparks.org/ReynoldsMansion)*

Palmetto Hall Plantation – *108 Fort Howell Dr.* - ☎*843-342-2582 - www. palmettohallgolf.com.* The Arthur Hills Course here alternates public/private every day until noon with its sister links, the Robert Cupp Course.

Hilton Head Tennis

Tennis is a popular pastime on Hilton Head, as the 300 courts on the island can testify. Below are a few of the eight clubs available for resort play.

Port Royal Golf and Racquet Club – *15 Wimbledon Ct., Port Royal Plantation* - ☎*843-686-8803 - www. portroyalgolfclub.com.* The Racquet Club features 10 clay courts and 4 hard-surface courts lit for night play.

Sea Pines Racquet Club – *5 Lighthouse Rd., Sea Pines* - ☎*843-363-4495 - www.seapines.com/ tennis.* This highly rated tennis club offers 23 clay courts and is home to the renowned Smith Stearns Tennis Academy.

Van Der Meer Shipyard Tennis Resort – *116 Shipyard Dr., Shipyard Plantation* - ☎*843-785-8388 - www. vandermeertennis.com.* Owned by tennis instructor **Dennis Van Der Meer**, this clinic-focused tennis resort boasts 20 championship courts, including the island's only covered and indoor courts.

The **Van Der Meer Tennis Center** is also located on Hilton Head Island *(19 Deallyon Ave.* - ☎*843-785-8388 - www.vandermeertennis.com)* and offers 17 hard-surface courts, 4 of which are covered and lit.

HUNTING ISLAND STATE PARK ★

00 *2555 Sea Island Pkwy.,16mi east of Beaufort via US-21 South* - ☎*843-838-2011 - southcarolinaparks.com - Open year-round daily 6am-6pm (until 9pm during Daylight Saving Time) - $5 adults, $3 children (ages 6-15).* True to its name, this beautiful barrier island was once used as a hunting ground. Now it's a 5,000-acre recreation spot that is South Carolina's most popular state park, attracting more than one million visitors each year. Palmetto trees and semi-tropical maritime forest edge the four miles of pristine beach. Anglers can cast their lines off the **fishing pier** (on the southern part of the island), which extends 1,120 feet into Fripp Inlet. Nature lovers can walk the park's trails and look for sea horses in the man-made lagoon, or try to catch a glimpse of pelicans, egrets, oystercatchers and wood storks that frequent this area. If you can't tear yourself away, reserve one of the park's 200 campsites (two-night minimum) or its lone cabin.

Red Piano Too Art Gallery

870 Sea Island Pkwy./US-21 - ☎*843-838-2241 - www.redpianotoo.com - Open Mon-Sat 10am-5pm, Sun 1pm-4:30pm. A trip to St. Helena Island isn't complete without a visit to this gallery. A local enclave for Gullah art, the c.1940s structure is packed with paintings, sculpture and folk art by 150 Southern self-taught artists. You'll get a good feel for Gullah culture here.*

Lighthouse, Hunting Island State Park

© DiscoverSouthCarolina.com

Lighthouse

Open year-round daily 10am-4:45pm - Nov-Feb until 3:45pm - $2.
Confederate forces destroyed the 1859 lighthouse that once stood here so the Union army couldn't use it as a navigation aid. Rebuilt in 1875 (and renovated in 2003), the light towers 170 feet above the inlet. Climb the 167 steps to the observation deck for a panorama of the heavily forested island and the expansive Atlantic Ocean stretching endlessly to the north and to the south.

WILD DUNES★

15mi north of Charleston on Isle of Palms via US-17 North to the Isle of Palms Connector (Rte. 517) -
☎866-359-5593 - *www.destination hotels.com/wilddunes.*
Bounded by the Intracoastal Waterway on one side and the Atlantic Ocean on the other, Wild Dunes sprawls out over acres of salt marsh, tidal creeks and two miles of white-sand beach at the northern tip of **Isle of Palms★**.
Long before a bridge connected this barrier island to the mainland, the Seewee Indians called the island home. The first resort was built here in 1972 when the Sea Pines Company (which developed Hilton Head) built the Isle of Palms Beach and Racquet Club on 1,600 acres of land at the north end of the island. New owners added a Tom Fazio-designed golf course (Wild Dunes Links) in 1980, and four years later the resort's name was changed to Wild Dunes Beach and Racquet Club.
Accommodations here today range from the 93-room **Boardwalk Inn** (🕭*see p. 138*) to a wide variety of rental properties, including houses and condominiums.

Resort Activities

Wild Dunes claims 36 holes of **championship golf** on two courses (🕭*see p. 154*), both open to the public. One of the holes on the Links Course has a fascinating history. During the Revolutionary War, a cadre of 2,000 men under the command of Britain's Lord Cornwallis landed on Isle of Palms intending to cross Breach Inlet to Sullivans Island and launch a surprise attack on Fort Moultrie. The place where they made landfall is now the Links' 18th hole.

The **tennis center** here has a full-service pro shop plus 17 Har-Tru courts, 5 of which are lit for night games. Wild Dunes has been rated among the top 10 tennis resorts in the US by *Tennis Magazine* for nine years in a row. In addition to golf and tennis, you can choose from working out at the fitness center, having a spa treatment, boating and taking kayak tours and wildlife excursions. Planned morning activities amuse the little ones (ages 5 and up) in summer. Teens can rent paddleboards and kayaks at the **Isle of Palms Marina** *(50 41st Ave. - 𝒫843-886-0209)*.

PENN CENTER NATIONAL HISTORIC LANDMARK DISTRICT

16 Penn Center Circle W., 6.3mi southeast of Beaufort on St. Helena Island via US-21 - 𝒫843-838-2432 - www.penncenter.com.
Not far from Beaufort, this historic complex makes a worthwhile excursion. Now used as a conference center, the 19 buildings here recall the school established in 1862 by Philadelphia Quakers Laura Towne and Ellen Murray to educate Sea Island slaves freed at the beginning of the Civil War, before emancipation.

York W. Bailey Museum

16 Penn Center Circle W., St. Helena Island. 𝒫843-838-2474. Open year-round Mon–Sat 9am–4pm. Closed Sun and major holidays. $5 adults, children $3 (ages 6-16). Preserving Sea Island culture and history, the museum highlights photographs and rare African artifacts.

SAVANNAH★★

Tourist information: 10 E. Bay St. - 𝒫912-644-6400 or 𝒫877-728-2662 - www.visitsavannah.com.
It's only a couple of hours down the coast from Charleston to the quintessentially Southern city of Savannah, with its landscaped squares, stately mansions, Spanish-moss-draped live oaks and eccentric ways.
The city was born in 1733 when English army officer and philanthropist **James Oglethorpe** and a group of more than 100 settlers landed at Yamacraw Bluff above the Savannah River.
One of 21 trustees to whom King George II had granted the tract of land between the Savannah and Altamaha rivers, Oglethorpe envisioned the colony of Georgia as a place where the British working poor and "societal misfits" could carve

91

Touring Tip

Stop first at the **Savannah Visitor Center** (301 Martin Luther King Jr. Blvd. - 𝒫912-944-0455 - www.visit-historic-savannah.com - open year-round daily 9am-5:30pm), where you can catch one of the narrated trolley tours of the historic downtown. For a quick overview of the city's past, visit the adjoining **Savannah History Museum** (912-651-6825 - www.chsgeorgia.org - open year-round daily 9am-5:30pm - closed Jan 1, Thanksgiving Day & Dec 25 - $7 adults, $4 children ages 2-12).

© SeanPavonePhoto/ iStock

out a living cultivating agricultural products desired by the Crown. In its early years, the region's economy, based on rice and tobacco, and later, cotton, fueled Savannah's growth as a port and a center for commodities trading. By 1817 Savannah's City Exchange was setting the market price for the world's cotton.

That all ended with the Civil War. When General Sherman reached Savannah in December 1864, city leaders surrendered without a fight. Sherman, acknowledging the city's beauty, presented Savannah to President Abraham Lincoln as a Christmas present.

Southern charm now pervades this bluff-top city—a testimony to

St. Patrick's Day in Savannah

You might think it's Mardi Gras when you see Savannah's St. Patrick's Day celebration. The squares aren't the only things that are green on March 17. The water in the fountains and the beer in the bars are dyed green too. The celebration began in 1813 with the Irish Hibernian Society. The 2-hour parade and the River Street bacchanalia that follows attract hearty partygoers from around the country. For details, go online to www. savannahsaintpatricksday.com.

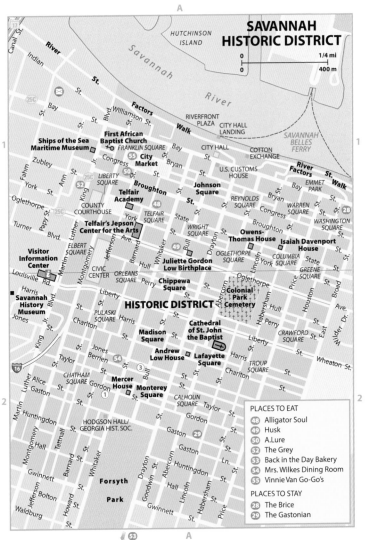

SAVANNAH HISTORIC DISTRICT

0   1/4 mi
0   400 m

93

PLACES TO EAT
48 Alligator Soul
49 Husk
50 A.Lure
52 The Grey
53 Back in the Day Bakery
54 Mrs. Wilkes Dining Room
55 Vinnie Van Go-Go's

PLACES TO STAY
28 The Brice
29 The Gastonian

© J. Arnold Images / hemis.fr

Forsyth Park

visionary 18C city planning and modern historic preservation.

HISTORIC DISTRICT★★

Bounded by Gwinnett St., E. Broad St., Martin Luther King Jr. Blvd. and the river.
James Oglethorpe's revered original city plan incorporated a perfect grid of broad thoroughfares punctuated by 24 grassy **squares** (three have been lost to urban sprawl). Bull Street cuts down the center of the grid, extending from 20-acre **Forsyth Park★**, with its graceful fountain, to the gold-domed City Hall.
Edged with handsome 19C examples of Greek Revival, Federal, Regency and Georgian architecture, Oglethorpe's streets and squares are now preserved in the 2.5-mile downtown historic district.

Factors Walk★★

West Factors Walk lines Bay St. between Whitaker and Montgomery Sts. East Factors Walk is on Bay St. between Lincoln and Houston Sts.
Riverfront warehouses along Bay Street make up the area known as Factors Walk, which was the hub of the cotton commerce in the 19C. Here cotton traders, called factors, would buy and sell from the bridgeways that connect the offices on the upper portion of the bluff—the two-story buildings that face Bay Street—with

the warehouses on cobblestone **River Street** below.

If you walk down the steep steps to River Street, you'll discover that the now-restored 19C warehouses contain a dizzying array of shops, galleries and restaurants. You'll find souvenir shops, candy stores, art galleries, and even a Christmas shop and an open-air market with some 75 vendors.

Owens-Thomas House★★

124 Abercorn St. - ✆912-790-8800 - www.telfair.org - Visit by 45-minute guided tour only, year-round Mon noon-5pm, Tue-Sat 10am-5pm, Sun and Mon noon-5pm (last tour at 4:20pm) - Closed major holidays - $20 combination ticket includes Telfair Academy and Jepson Center.

The belle of Oglethorpe Square, the Owens-Thomas House is considered one of architect William Jay's finest works—and the only unaltered

© J. Arnold Images/hemis.fr

Factor's Walk **95**

City Hall

Separating East and West Factors Walk, 1905 City Hall (2 E. Bay St. at Bull St.) reigns as a vibrant local landmark with its 70-foot-high dome, covered in 23-karat gold leaf. City Hall stands on the site of the Old City Exchange, which set the market price for the world's cotton in the days before the Civil War. A marble bench in front of the building commemorates Oglethorpe's landing on this bluff in 1733.

example of his surviving designs. Now administered by the **Telfair Academy★** (&see p. 98) this house was completed in 1819 for cotton merchant Richard Richardson when the architect was only 25. The stately structure typifies the English Regency style. Its exterior is composed of tabby and coadestone, while the interior is adorned with Duncan Phyfe furniture and a brass-inlaid staircase. Out back, the carriage house includes one of the earliest intact urban slave quarters in the South.

Andrew Low House★

329 Abercorn St. - ☎912-233-6854 - www.andrewlowhouse.com - Visit by 30-minute guided tour only, year-round Mon-Sat 10am-4pm, Sun noon-4pm - Closed major holidays and first 2 weeks Jan - $10. In 1848 wealthy cotton merchant Andrew Low commissioned John Norris to create this Classical-style house with its elaborate cast-iron balconies. Low's

son, William, married Savannah-born **Juliette Gordon Low** (1860–1927), who founded the Girl Scouts here on March 12, 1912. Located in back of the residence, the Lows' carriage house served as the first headquarters of the Girl Scouts USA—the world's largest voluntary organization for girls. Juliette Gordon Low died at Low House in 1927. Today Low family pieces and period antiques fill the rooms.

Cathedral of St. John the Baptist★

222 E. Harris St. - ☎912-233-4709 - www.savannahcathedral.org - Open year-round Mon-Sat 9am-11:45am and 12:45pm-5pm - $2 donation requested. You'll recognize the seat of Savannah's Catholic diocese by the twin spires that tower over the historic district. Dedicated in 1876, this French Gothic cathedral dates back to a parish established in Savannah in the late 1700s. Step inside to see the results of the four-year restoration (completed in 2000) that returned the cathedral's Austrian stained-glass windows, slate roof and Italian marble altar to their former glory.

Isaiah Davenport House★

324 E. State St. - ☎912-236-8097 - www.davenporthousemuseum.org - Visit by 40-minute guided tour only, year-round Mon-Sat 10am-4pm, Sun 1pm-4pm (last tour 4pm) - Closed major holidays - $9. Designed by Rhode Island master builder Isaiah Davenport, this two-story brick Federal structure was completed in

© D. K. Johnson/ Getty Images

Mercer Williams House

1820. When threatened by demolition in the 1950s, community efforts saved it and established the Historic Savannah Foundation, a grassroots organization that has been key in rejuvenating the historic district.

Mercer Williams House★

429 Bull St. - ☏912-236-6352 - www. mercerhouse.com - Visit by 30-minute guided tour only, year-round Mon-Sat 10:30am-4:10pm, Sun noon-4pm. $12.50 - Purchase tickets at the Mercer House Carriage Shop at 430 Whitaker St. (Mon-Sat 10am-5pm, Sun 10:30am-4:30pm). A stately Italianate mansion overlooking Monterey Square, the c.1868 residence designed by New York architect John

Norris—became famous as a crime scene. It was in this house in 1981 that resident antiques dealer Jim Williams was accused of fatally shooting 21-year-old Danny Hansford. Williams' murder trial set staid Savannah on its ear, and was later immortalized in John Berendt's best-selling 1994 book *Midnight in the Garden of Good and Evil.* Both the book and the movie that followed in 1997 painted a vivid picture of Savannah's eccentric populace. The most recognized icon from the book is, perhaps, the sculpture *Bird Girl* (1938), which appears on the book's cover. The work of Sylvia Shaw Judson, the statue stands in the Telfair Academy.

Ships of the Sea Maritime Museum★

41 Martin Luther King Jr. Blvd. - ☎912-232-1511 - www.shipsofthesea.org - Open year-round Tue-Sun 10am-5pm (last admission 4:15pm) - Closed Mon and major holidays - $9 adult, $7 children, under age 6 free.

A block west of City Market, a charming garden invites visitors into Scarbrough House, an 1819 Regency villa designed by famed English architect William Jay. Today the villa houses a maritime museum, which presents nautical history and Savannah's seafaring culture through artifacts, paintings and model ships from early days of sail to World War II.

Telfair Academy★

121 Barnard St. - ☎912-790-8800 - www.telfair.org - Open year-round Sun-Mon noon-5pm, Tue-Sat 10am-5pm - Closed major holidays. $20 combination ticket includes entry to Owens-Thomas House and Jepson Center - ♿. Another creation of William Jay, the Regency-style mansion was built in 1818 as the home of Alexander Telfair. The expanded structure now houses 19C and 20C American and European paintings and portraiture, including works by members of the Ash Can school—Robert Henri, George Luks and George Bellows.

Located on the entrance level was Telfair's reception room, the **Octagon Room**, with its 19C Grecian couches and faux oak paneling; and the **Dining Room**, showcasing a Duncan Phyfe mahogany sideboard and early 19C English silver.

Next door, the 64,000sq ft modern **Jepson Center** *(year-round Sun–Mon noon–5pm, Tue–Sat 10am–5pm - closed major holidays - $20 combination ticket -* ♿*)* was designed for Telfair by renowned architect Moshe Safdie. It houses the academy's collection of 20C and 21C art, including a prestigious array of works on paper by major artists of the past 50 years.

Broughton Street Shopping

Interesting shops line Broughton Street from Bull Street to Martin Luther King Jr. Boulevard. Here are a few examples:

Paris Market and Brocante – *36 W. Broughton St. - ☎912-232-1500 - theparismarket. com. Quirky, unusual finds gleaned from across the globe.*

Go Fish – *106 W. Broughton St. - ☎912-234-1260 - www.shopgofish.com. The casual women's clothing here is made by indigenous people of developing nations.*

Clipper Trading Company – *115 W. Broughton St. - ☎912-238-3660. Furniture, crafts and gift items from across Asia.*

Zia Boutique – *325 W. Broughton St. - ☎912-233-3237 - www.ziaboutique.com. Exotic jewelry and gifts inspired by the Kenyan owner's world travels.*

City Market

Bounded by Bryan, Congress, Montgomery and Barnard Sts. - ☎912-232-4903 - www.savannah citymarket.com. At this lively open-air marketplace, you can listen to live music, catch a carriage tour, sample the shops or relax at the outdoor cafes. Among the goodies you'll find here are **Byrd's Famous Cookies** (in Savannah since 1924), Woof Gang Bakery for canine treats and toys, and the Pie Society, a traditional British bakery.

Across from the market, the **First African Baptist Church★** is considered the oldest black church in North America *(23 Montgomery St. - ☎912-233-6597 - www.firstafricanbc. com - tours Tue-Sat 10am, 2pm and 4pm, Sun 1pm - $10)*. Now a National Historic Landmark, the church was founded by freed slave George Leile in 1773. The current structure was built in 1859 by the congregation.

Colonial Park Cemetery

200 Abercorn St., entrance at Abercorn and E. Oglethorpe Sts. - ☎912-651-6843 - Open Mar-Nov daily 8am-8pm (rest of the year until 5pm). Savannah's second cemetery opened in 1750; the last body was buried here in 1853. Tucked amid the live oaks are the graves of James Habersham, acting Royal Governor of the Province of Georgia from 1771–73; naval hero Captain Denis Cottineau, who fought with John Paul Jones in 1779; and renowned 18C miniaturist Edward Greene Malbone. The cemetery has been a park since 1896.

Juliette Gordon Low Birthplace

10 E. Oglethorpe Ave. - ☎912-233-4501 - www.juliettegordonlowbirthplace. org - Open Feb-Dec Mon-Sat 10am-5pm - Closed Jan and major holidays - $15 adults, $12 children (ages 5-18) - Guided tours available - ♿. The founder of the Girl Scouts was born in this house in 1860. Known as Daisy, Low was the second of six children of cotton factor William Gordon II and his wife, Eleanor. The 1821 English Regency-style house has been painstakingly restored to reflect the year 1886, when Juliette Gordon married William Mackay Low.

FORT PULASKI NATIONAL MONUMENT★

14mi east of downtown Savannah via US-80, on Tybee Island - ☎912-786-8182 - www.nps.gov/fopu - Open year-round daily 9am-5pm - Closed Jan 1, Thanksgiving Day, Dec 25 - $7 adults, under 16 free.
Named for Revolutionary War hero **Casimir Pulaski**, who lost his life defending the city of Savannah against the British, Fort Pulaski was built between 1833 and 1847. The battery saw most of its action during the Civil War, when Confederate troops laid siege to the fort before Georgia seceded from the Union. In April 1862, Union forces recaptured the fort, using their experimental rifled cannon. They quickly sealed off the port of Savannah and held Fort Pulaski for the rest of the war. In 1924 Fort Pulaski was declared a national monument. Today you can

Fort Pulaski National Monument with moat

tour its restored ramparts, complete with cannon, moat and drawbridge. The 5,600-acre site includes picnic grounds and nature trails, with views of the Atlantic Ocean in the distance.

GEORGIA'S GOLDEN ISLES★

70 miles south of Savannah via I-95 and US-17 South - Tourist information: ☏912-265-0620 or ☏800-933-2627 - www.goldenisles.com.

Strung like shining beads along Georgia's Atlantic Coast, the Golden Isles—Sea Island, St. Simons Island, private Little St. Simons Island and Jekyll Island—lie amid a setting of gold-green marshes, diamond-white sands and lapis-blue waters. These popular islands boast an average

annual temperature of 68°F and attract thousands of visitors each year to play on the area's golf courses and tennis courts, visit its historic resorts, and relax on its wide sandy beaches.

CUMBERLAND ISLAND NATIONAL SEASHORE★★

10mi southeast of Brunswick in St. Mary's GA (take I-95 South to Rte 40) - Accessible by ferry (45 minutes) only from downtown St. Marys - Reservations required (⊙*see p. 101) - ☏912-882-4336 - www.nps.gov/cuis.*

A haven for wild horses, sea turtles, alligators, armadillos and a host of shorebirds, Cumberland Island National Seashore sprawls over

The Scoop on Cumberland Island

Getting to Cumberland Island – *Stop for information at the Cumberland Island Visitor Center on the mainland in St. Marys (113 St. Marys St. - ☎912-882-4336 - open year-round daily 8am-4pm - closed Dec 25). Ferries leave from 107 St. Marys St. - ☎912-882-4336 - www.cumberlandislandferry.com - round-trip $28 adults, $18 children ages 15 and under - reservations suggested - Check-in 30 minutes prior to departure. Park entrance fee to visit the island is $7 (valid 7 consecutive days). No supplies are available on the island.*

Getting around – *Land and Legacies 6-hour guided van tours cover much of the island and give access to Plum Orchard (available only from 9am ferry - reservations required - ☎877-860-6787 - $45/person). Other than van tours, bicycles and walking are the only means of getting around. Bikes are available for rent at Sea Camp (☎912-882-4336 - $16/day).*

Camping – *Reservations (☎912-882-4335) are required for camping on the island, limited to 7 days. Wilderness sites ($9/person/night) have no facilities; water should be treated. Campfires are not permitted. Sea Camp ($22/person/night) and Stafford campgrounds ($12/person/night) have restrooms and cold showers (Sea Camp also has treated drinking water). Each campsite has a grill, fire ring, food cage and picnic tables.*

Cumberland Island National Seashore

© epicurean/iStockphoto.com

102

Brunswick Stew

First created in Brunswick, Georgia—the commercial hub of the Golden Isles and an important port in its own right—delectable Brunswick stew combines chicken, beef and pork, slow-simmered with local vegetables (tomatoes, butter beans, corn, potatoes and okra), herbs and spices. It's often served with fresh local shrimp, crab and oysters, and appears on many menus throughout the area. Be sure to sample some while you're in the area.

17.5 miles of saltwater marshes, maritime forests and lonely beaches. The largest and least developed of Georgia's barrier islands lies across Cumberland Sound from St. Marys, Georgia. Several cotton plantations operated on the island before Thomas Carnegie (brother of Pittsburgh industrialist Andrew Carnegie) and his wife, Lucy, purchased 4,000 acres here in 1881. The secluded estate they constructed in 1884 was used for hunting and for entertaining guests. The magnificent mansion burned down in 1959 (only the ruins remain today). Carnegie descendants owned the land until 1972, when they donated most of it to the National Park Service.

Plum Orchard

7.5mi one-way from ferry landing - Visit by guided tour only - ☎912-882-4335. Georgian Revival-style Plum Orchard was built in 1898 for Thomas Carnegie's son, George, and his wife.

Visitors are invited to tour its partly furnished rooms.

Dungeness

The eerie ruins of the mansion Thomas and Lucy Carnegie completed in 1886 now rise amid the island foliage. In its heyday, the grand Queen Anne-style home boasted 59 rooms. After Carnegie's death, his wife, Lucy, continued to live here. The family finally moved out of Dungeness in 1925. The mansion was destroyed by fire 34 years later.

First African Baptist Church

North end of Cumberland Island. Fashioned from white-washed logs, this one-room church hosted quite the celebrity wedding, when John F. Kennedy Jr. and Carolyn Bessette married in secret, away from the eyes of the paparazzi. The 11 handmade pews inside seat only 40 people.

Greyfield Inn

South end of the island - ☎904-261-6408 - www.greyfieldinn.com. Another former Carnegie mansion, the rambling home built in 1900 for Margaret Ricketson, daughter of Thomas and Lucy Carnegie, now operates as an upscale inn—the island's only lodging.

JEKYLL ISLAND★★

From I-95, take Exit 29 and follow US-17 to Jekyll Island Causeway. The Visitor Information Center is located on the causeway (901 Downing Musgrove Pkwy.) - ☎912-635-3636 - www.jekyllisland.com - Open year-round Mon-Sat 9am-6pm, Sun

© J. Arnold images / hemis.fr

Driftwood Beach, Jekyll Island

10am-5pm - $6 daily pass to drive and park on the island (weekly pass $28) to drive onto the island.
Dubbed Georgia's Jewel, Jekyll Island grew up as a playground for America's millionaires. Men named Gould, Goodyear, Pulitzer and Rockefeller as well as other East Coast captains of industry formed a consortium in 1886 and purchased the island for $125,000. In 1887, consortium members—the self-proclaimed Jekyll Island Club—hired architect Charles Alexander to build a 60-room clubhouse (now the Jekyll Island Club Hotel). The wealthy industrialists soon supplemented their clubhouse with cottages, as they called their anything-but-modest

winter retreats, which ranged up to 8,000 square feet in size.
In 1942, World War II put an end to the playtime, and the club closed. Five years later, the State of Georgia purchased Jekyll Island, which today preserves the island's historic structures within the 240-acre historic district, now a National Historic Landmark. The ocean side of the island is lined with hotels and **unspoiled beaches**.

Jekyll Island National Historic District★★

Tours depart from the Jekyll Island Museum - 100 Stable Rd.; ℘912-635-4036 - www.jekyllisland.com - The 90-minute tram tour (daily 11am, 1pm and 3pm; $16) allows access to two historic cottages and Faith Chapel. To see the sights here, wander around at your leisure, or take a guided tram tour. The Queen Anne-style **Jekyll Island Club**, with its signature turret, has been restored as a resort hotel *(371 Riverview Dr.)*, along with the members' former cottages and outbuildings. Even the shops occupy historic structures: a bookstore fills what was once the infirmary; and the former powerhouse has been restored to house the **Georgia Sea Turtle Center** *(214 Stable Rd. - ☎912-635-4444 - gstc.jekyllisland. com - open daily 9am-5pm - closed Jan 1, Thanksgiving Day, Dec 24 and 25 - $8 adults, $6 children ages 4-12)*, a rehabilitation facility that is open to the public.

Cottages – Facing the Intracoastal Waterway amid moss-draped oaks, 15 cottages were built by club members beginning in 1887. At that time, decades before a bridge linked Jekyll Island to the mainland, members arrived for the season via steamship or private yacht.

Goodyear Cottage, built for lumber baron Frank Goodyear in 1906 *(☎912-635-3920 - open Mon-Fri noon-4pm, Sat-Sun 10am-4pm)* houses the **Jekyll Island Arts Association,** a gift shop and free monthly art exhibits. With 20 rooms and 13 baths, Italian Renaissance **Crane Cottage** (1917) was the grandest on the island. Crane and **Cherokee** (1904) cottages have both been restored as additions to the hotel.

Faith Chapel – *Open year-round daily 10am-4pm.* Constructed in 1904, this little wooden chapel once held religious services for the members of the Jekyll Island Club. Stop in to see the chapel's striking stained-glass windows, designed by Louis Comfort Tiffany and D. Maitland Armstrong.

ST. SIMONS ISLAND ★

77mi south of Savannah. From I-95, take Exit 9 and follow US-17 South to St. Simons Causeway.
Largest of the Golden Isles, St. Simons is known for its beautiful beaches as well as its colorful history. Beginning

Little St. Simons

Accessible only by boat from Hampton River Club Marina at the north end of St. Simons Island - Day-trip packages ($95 per person) include transportation, naturalist-guided tours, lunch and beach time - By advance reservations only - ☎888-733-5774 - www.littlestsimonsisland.com. Eleven thousand acres of pristine natural beauty compose private Little St. Simons Island. No crowds disturb this tranquil birder's paradise. Purchased for its cedar trees in the early 1900s by pencil manufacturer Philip Berolzheimer, Little St. Simons now offers accommodations in six cottages, including the three-bedroom Helen House. Accommodations are limited to only 32 overnight guests at a time. Canoe the tidal creeks, bike the 15 miles of trails, or stroll the seven miles of deserted beach.

in 1736, when James Oglethorpe built Fort Frederica here, the English and Spanish struggled for control of the island. Oglethorpe attempted unsuccessfully to capture the Spanish fort in St. Augustine, Florida, in 1740; the Spanish counterattack came two years later. During the **Battle of Bloody Marsh** in 1742, Oglethorpe and his forces soundly defeated the Spaniards, who retreated back to Florida (a small monument off Demere Road marks the battle site). In the years before the Civil War, St. Simons was blanketed with cotton plantations, known for their high-quality Sea Island cotton. Now resort hotels and golf clubs cover much of the former plantation land.

The tiny **village** of St. Simons Island at the southern tip centers on Mallery Street *(off Kings Way/Ocean Blvd.)*, where you'll find shops and restaurants, as well as the public pier *(end of Mallery St.)*.

Fort Frederica National Monument★

At the end of Frederica Rd. - ☎912-638-3639 - www.nps.gov/fofr. Grounds open year-round daily 9am-5pm. Closed Jan 1, Thanksgiving Day and Dec 25. James Oglethorpe and his soldiers built Fort Frederica in 1736 as Georgia's first military outpost. Today the ruins of the square fort and its earthen ramparts stand on a bend in the Frederica River.

St. Simons Island Light

610 Beachview Dr. - ☎912-638-4666 - www.saintsimonslighthouse.org - Open year-round Mon-Sat 10am-5pm, Sun 1:30pm-5pm (last climb 4:30

daily) - Closed major holidays - $12 adults, $5 children (ages 6-12). Icon of the island, this 104-foot-tall working lighthouse stands near the pier, where it has guided sailors since 1872. Climb the 129 steps for a great view of the Golden Isles. The restored Keepers Dwelling offers glimpses into area history, and artifacts from the area's seafaring past are on exhibit in the Lighthouse Museum *(open Mon-Sat 10am-5pm, Sun 1:30pm-5pm)*.

SEA ISLAND

Accessible via Sea Island Dr. from St. Simons Island.
Ohio automobile magnate Howard Coffin had a vision as he looked out across the undeveloped marshland of Sea Island in 1923. In his mind's eye, he imagined a resort and beachfront homes on the land that once held cotton plantations.

Coffin's dream is a reality today. Sea Island, with its residential cottage community, is synonymous with **The Cloister,** a world-class resort *(entrance off Sea Island Dr.)* that occupies part of the island.

Addresses

Georgia Sea Grill
©Georgia Sea Grill/h2o creative group

Where to eat

There's no mistake that Charleston consistently wins accolades as one of the country's best food cities. in fact, the list of local chefs that have been nominated for, or won, coveted James Beard Awards is too numerous to mention. You'll find all types of cuisine in Charleston, but the most typical fare is Southern with Lowcountry accents.

The venues listed below were selected for their ambiance, location and/or value for money. Rates indicate the average cost of an appetizer, an entrée and a dessert for one person (not including tax, gratuity or beverages). Most restaurants are open daily for lunch and dinner (except where noted) and accept major credit cards. Call for information regarding reservations, dress code and opening hours.

ⓖ Find the addresses on our plans with numbered pads (ex. ①). The coordinates in red (eg C2) refer to the detachable plane.

CHARLESTON HISTORIC DISTRICT

Over $75

① **Charleston Grill** – *E6* – *224 King St., in Belmond Charleston Place hotel* - *☎843-577-4522 - www. charlestongrill.com - Dinner only.* Chef Michelle Weaver continues to win raves at Charleston Grill, where live jazz, cream-colored leather seating and mahogany-paneled walls set the stage for a meal to remember. Dishes are divided into four categories. Social and Shared lists starters for the table, while Roots and Stems highlights local vegetables. Waves and Marsh shows off the bounty of area waters (including Weaver's renowned crab cakes), and «Field and Pasture» carves out heartier meat dishes.

② **McCrady's** – *F6* – *2 Unity Alley - Dinner only - Closed Mon & Tue - mccradysrestaurant.com.* Adjacent to McCrady's Tavern, Southern culinary legend Sean Brock's new tasting-menu-only restaurant fulfills his lifelong dream. Diners must purchase tickets online well in advance for the sought-after seatings in this chic and intimate 22-seat space. Expect a cascade of amazing contemporary small courses to come from the open induction kitchen in this two-hour-plus experience, which the chef infuses with flavors from his travels around the world.

$50-$75

③ **82 Queen** – *E6* – *82 Queen St. - ☎843-723-7591 - www.82queen.com - Lunch Mon-Fri - Dinner daily - Brunch Sat & Sun.* Charleston's special-occasion restaurant since 1982 sits in the heart of the Historic District. Its two attached 19C row houses, connected by a shady courtyard, contain 11 romantic dining rooms.

© Andrew Cebulka/Polished Pig Media

109

McCrady's

Award-winning she-crab soup, Carolina crab cakes, barbecue shrimp and grits, and Charleston bouillabaisse highlight the Lowcountry cuisine here.

④ **FIG** – *E6* – *232 Meeting St. - ☎843-805-5900 - eatatfig.com - Dinner only - Closed Sun.* Food is good at this Charleston standard—thus the acronym for FIG's name. In the elegantly understated dining room, seasonal fare by James Beard Award-winners Mike Lata and Jason Stanhope may include local roasted snowy grouper and a veal chop "saltimbocca," while the fish stew Provençale—in an aromatic saffron-scented broth—has been a menu fixture since day one.

⑤ **Fulton Five**– *E6* – *5 Fulton St. - ☎843-853-5555 - www.fultonfive charleston.com - Dinner only - Closed Sun.* Sage-green walls and crisp white tablecloths greet visitors to this cozy dining room, where Northern Italian fare rules. The seasonally changing menu might feature chocolate- and espresso-rubbed beef filet, and a traditional ragu *alla Bolognese.* The *pesce del giorno* (fish of the day) nets a different preparation daily. One thing is for sure: high-quality imported ingredients—prosciutto, olive oil, fine cheeses and aged balsamic vinegar—make a meal you won't quickly forget.

🍴

6 Husk – *E6* – *76 Queen St.* - *☏843-577-2500* - *huskrestaurant.com.* The second Charleston restaurant by James Beard Award-winner Sean Brock (the original McCrady's was his first) pays homage to the South in ingredients sourced from below the Mason-Dixon Line. The dining room, which occupies an 1893 house, echoes the Lowcountry in soft colors and natural design elements. Brock puts a contemporary spin on top-notch ingredients from the best local farms and food purveyors, and his cuisine sings with layers of carefully constructed flavors. Don't pass up a skillet of the wonderful cornbread.

7 Peninsula Grill – *E6* – *112 N. Market St., at the Planters Inn* - *☏843-723-0700* - *www.peninsulagrill.com* - *Dinner only.* Opened in 1987, the Peninsula Grill keeps diners coming back with good food and matching service in a romantic dining room, accented with velvet-covered walls. A crisp, cold wedge of Gem lettuce topped with fire-roasted tomatoes, Stilton cheese and buttermilk dressing makes a good prelude to pan-roasted sea scallops with diced lobster. The signature seven-layer coconut cake is a meal in itself. If you don't have room to try it, the restaurant will be glad to ship one to you.

8 Slightly North of Broad – *F6* – *192 E. Bay St.* - *☏843-723-3424* - *www.snobcharleston.com* - *Lunch Mon-Fri, Dinner daily, Brunch Sat & Sun.* Humor resides within the walls of this 19C brick warehouse, whose current tenant takes its

tongue-in-cheek name from its less-than-coveted location (historically, the best place to live in Charleston was south of Broad Street). It's no mistake that the restaurant's acronym spells SNOB. Songs of the South ring out in a Heritage Farm pork chop with local Mepkin Abbey mushroom farrotto, and the shrimp and grits made with South Carolina shrimp, Geechie Boys grits, house-made sausage and country ham.

$25-$50

9 Cru Cafe – *E6* – *18 Pinckney St.* - *☏843-534-2434* - *www.crucafe.com* - *Closed Sun & Mon.* Chef John Zucker dishes up some of the tastiest food in the Lowcountry inside an 18C single house. Favorites range from Thai seafood risotto to Chinese chicken salad, and the café is famed for its four-cheese macaroni. Expect to wait if you don't have a reservation—even at lunchtime.

10 Gaulart & Maliclet – *E7* – *98 Broad St.* - *☏843-577-9797* - *fastandfrenchcharleston.com* - *Closed Sun.* «Fast and French» is the motto—and the local moniker—of this small eatery. Pull up a stool at the communal counter and make a new friend. Daily lunch and dinner specials include a discounted glass of wine to promote the convivial atmosphere. Dinner entrées range from seafood Normandy to chicken Provençal. Go on Thursday for the selection of traditional fondues.

© Squire Fox/Polished Pig Media

Husk

11 Hank's Seafood Restaurant –
E6 10 Hayne St. - ☎843-723-3474 -
hanksseafoodrestaurant.com -
Dinner only. Hank's classy dining
room has risen to local stardom since
it appeared on the scene in 1999.
After you whet your appetite with
the award-winning she-crab soup or
an oyster sampler from the raw bar,
you'll have to choose between such
tantalizing house specialties as roast
grouper with tomato balsamic brown
butter, and a standout shrimp and
grits.

12 Le Farfalle – *E6* – 15 Beaufain St. -
☎843-212-0920 - *lefarfallecharleston.
com* - *No lunch Sat.* Pasta rules at Chef
Michael Toscano's year-old restaurant
in Harleston Village, just a couple of

blocks off King St. Octopus carpaccio
with pickled eggplant is hard to resist
to start. And you might be so taken
with toasted angel hair with scallops,
bacon, and braised leeks or the ricotta
gnudi with sweet Italian sausage that
you don't even bother to consider the
short list of entrées.

13 McCrady's Tavern – *F6* –
Unity Alley - ☎843-577-0025 -
mccradystavern.com - *Dinner &
weekend brunch.* Cozy as the colonial
tavern—Charleston's first—it started
as in 1778, this newly rebranded
restaurant tucks into a little alley
off East Bay Street. Old English
style reigns with timbered ceilings,
wrought-iron light fixtures, a wood-
burning fireplace and original brick

walls. Oysters McCrady (baked with country ham and mushrooms) and a grilled pork Porterhouse with melted onions illustrate the restaurant's irresistible modern take on tavern fare.

Under $25

14 **Breizh Pan' Crêpes** – *E6* – *39 George St. - ☏843-822-3313 - www.breizhpancrepes.com - Mon & Wed-Fri 8am-4pm, Sat 9am-3pm, Sun 9:30am-2pm - Closed Tue.* The highest quality French ingredients go into these authentic crêpes bretonnes, made to order by owner Patrice Rombaut and his wife, Celine. Savory versions include ham, Swiss cheese and egg, as well as chicken, and mushrooms and cream. Dessert crêpes are filled with the likes of pears and Chantilly cream, and Nutella and bananas. Gluten-free buckwheat crêpes are available.

15 **Minero** – *F6* – *155 E. Bay St.- ☏843-789-2241 - minerorestaurant.com - Closed Sun.* At this bustling second-floor taqueria, Chef Sean Brock (of Husk) offers his elevated spin on Mexican street food. Three hand-picked varieties of corn are ground daily using a traditional process to make the fresh masa (corn flour) that goes into Minero's tortillas. Fried catfish, pork carnitas, and grilled steak with heirloom peppers number among the taco options. Tequila and mezcal head the beverage list.

UPPER KING

$50-$75

16 **The MacIntosh** – *D5* – *479 King St. - ☏843-789-4299 - themacintosh charleston.com - Dinner & Sun brunch.* This popular spot fashions a lively, industrial-chic lair with its exposed ductwork. In the kitchen, chef/partner Jeremiah Bacon changes his menu to reflect the best of the season. That might mean short rib cappelletti with and house-made ricotta gnudi with white truffles. The Certified Angus Beef burger and the deckle steak are menu staples.

17 **The Ordinary** – *D4* – *544 King St. - ☏843-414-7060 - eattheordinary.com - Dinner only - Closed Mon.* Depending on what you order, it's deceptively easy to run up a big tab inside this beautifully renovated 1927 bank building. Chef Mike Lata's menu hies to small plates, and you might find yourself getting carried away between selections from the oyster bar and terrific small-plate options such as crispy oyster sliders, jumbo lump blue crab toast, and BBQ white shrimp. Daily specials run from fish schnitzel to lobster rolls.

$25-$50

18 **The Darling Oyster Bar** – *D5* *513 King St. - ☏843-641-0821 - thedarling.com - Dinner only.* The best seats in this handsome late-19C building are the 14 stools surrounding the U-shaped marble raw bar that faces King Street. Make your selection from the day's menu of oysters, sourced from the east and west coasts. Or go for one of the house specialties, like the King crab parfait or the daily ceviche. There are tables too, where you can order a fry basket or the daily fresh catch from the main menu.

19 The Grocery – *D4* – *4 Cannon St. - ☎843-302-8825 - wwwthegrocery charleston.com - Dinner only & Sun brunch - Closed Mon.* Shelves lined with colorful jars of pickles and preserves, all made in-house, set the tone for Chef Kevin Johnson's restaurant, steps off upper King Street. The appealing menu encourages sharing, with small plates of cornmeal-dusted oysters topped by a remarkable deviled-egg sauce. Among the changing entrées, you might find a roasted duck breast or a pan-roasted wreckfish with fennel cream.

20 Indaco – *D4* – *526 King St. - ☎864 -727-1228 - indacocharleston.com - Dinner only & Sun brunch.* Named with the Italian word for indigo, a crop that flourished in the Lowcountry in the early 19C, Indaco joins the parade of stellar restaurants on upper King. Rustic flavors pop in wood-fired pizzas as well as in the luscious short rib ravioli with black truffle, and the Sardinian seafood stew. Creative cocktails, craft beers and Italian wines highlight the in-house beverage program.

21 O-Ku – *D5* – *463 King St. - ☎843-737-0112 - o-kusushi.com.* In this chic contemporary space on upper King Street, sushi, crudo and creative makimono (sushi rolls) are made with the freshest fish from as far away as Norway and as close as local waters. Chef's specialties include local whitefish crudo, O-Ku spring rolls and lobster temaki. Can't decide? Order the multicourse omakase tasting menu and leave your meal up to the whims of the chef.

22 Trattoria Lucca – *D4* – *41 Bogard St. - ☎843-973-3323 - luccacharleston.com - Dinner only - Closed Sun.* Off the beaten track in the Elliotborough neighborhood, this cozy trattoria showcases the terrific cooking of Chef Ken Vedrinksi. House-made pastas (spaghettoni «Nero» with grilled Rhode Island calamari, nduja and parsley) are always a hit. But don't pass up plates—such as doormat flounder in a rye crust—that combine local ingredients with Italian flair. Come for the four-course family-style supper on Monday nights.

Under $25

23 Hominy Grill – *D5* – *207 Rutledge Ave. - ☎843-937-0930 - hominy grill.com - Mon-Fri 7:30am-3pm, Sat & Sun 9am-3pm.* The staff at Hominy Grill believes you are what you eat. So they get their produce from area farms, their fish from local waters and their grits from a water-powered mill in North Carolina. Hominy Grill occupies an 1897 single house in the Cannonborough neighborhood, where Chef Robert Stehling glazes pork belly with sorghum and smothers hicken Country Captain in a tomato curry sauce. Check the chalkboard for the day's homemade desserts.

🍴

NORTH MORRISON (NOMO)

Under $25

24 Lewis Barbecue – *D2* – *464 N. Nassau St.* - ☏*843-805-9500 - lewisbarbecue.com - Closed Mon.* Texas barbecue, cooked for hours in custom-made smokers and cut to order, brings 'em back for more at John Lewis' Charleston barbecue joint off Morrison Avenue (the continuation of East Bay Street). Go for the signature Prime beef brisket—it melts in your mouth—and the Texas hot guts, the chef's house-made sausage, with a side of green-chile corn pudding.

25 Martha Lou's Kitchen – *D2* *1068 Morrison Dr.* - ☏*843-577-9583. marthalouskitchen.com - Mon-Sat 11am-6pm - Closed Sun.* Owner Martha Lou Gadsden does comfort food right in this little hot-pink house near the foot of the Ravenel Bridge. Locals come to her no-frills, meat-and-three place for the best Southern fried chicken in town. All main courses here come with a choice of two or three sides, including cornbread, lima beans and mac and cheese. Cash only.

☾ *The following restaurants are off map.*

OFF THE PENINSULA

$50-$75

Coda del Pesce – *1130 Ocean Blvd., Isle of Palms.* ☏*843-242-8570 - codadelpesce.com - Dinner only - Closed Sun.* Chef Ken Vedrinski of Charleston's Trattoria Lucca brings his talent to Isle of Palms at this oceanfront restaurant. Reclaimed wood and picture windows overlooking the Atlantic set a beachy scene on the second floor, where Italian accents pepper dishes such as local flounder braciole and picatta of local swordfish «Torcino-style.» After the meal, house-made gelato is difficult to pass up.

$25-$50

The Boathouse at Breach Inlet - *101 Palm Blvd., Isle of Palms* - ☏*843-886-8000 - www.boathouse restaurants.com - Dinner daily & Sun brunch.* There's always a crowd at this waterfront seafood place. The restaurant's mantra «simply fresh seafood» means that fresh local fish such as black grouper and red snapper are grilled and come with your choice of sauces and sides. Signature seafood combinations mix crab cakes, steak and butter-poached lobster tails. Watch the sunset over Breach Inlet from your table or from the rooftop Crow's Nest Bar.

NICO – *201 Coleman Blvd., Mt. Pleasant* - ☏*843-352-7969 - nicoshemcreek.com - Dinner only.* Just over the Ravenel Bridge from downtown Charleston, Chef Nico Romo's new restaurant highlights local seafood with a French twist. A raw bar menu, featuring a selection of fresh oysters, supplements entrées from the wood-fired oven. For something different, try the quenelle, a traditional dish from Lyon, France, that presents a delicate fish dumpling bathed in a creamy Nantua sauce and garnished with crayfish.

Obstinate Daughter – *2063 Middle St., Sullivans Island -* ☎*843-416-5020 - www.theobstinatedaughter.com - Lunch Mon-Fri - Dinner daily - Brunch Sat & Sun.* This restaurant's name pays homage to the Revolutionary War history of Sullivans Island, while the food spotlights the talents of Chef Jacques Larson. Share small plates of griddled octopus and roasted beets before diving into thin-crust pizza or a plate of homemade lemon pappardelle pasta with lobster, shrimp, fennel and roasted tomatoes.

Red Drum Gastropub – *803 Coleman Blvd., Mt. Pleasant -* ☎*843-849-0313 - reddrumrestaurant.com - Dinner daily - Brunch Sat & Sun.* It's well worth a trip across the Cooper River for a meal at the Red Drum, where chef/owner Ben Berryhill uses Southwestern accents to spike wood-grilled chicken with Mexican cheese, avocado relish and garlic cream. Appetizers offer a taste of the American Southwest with the likes of crabmeat tostaditas and blistered padron peppers. The brick patio is great for outdoor dining.

THE GRAND STRAND

$50-$75

Chive Blossom Cafe – *85 N. Causeway Rd., Pawleys Island -* ☎*843-237-1438 - www.chiveblossom.com - Closed Sun.* With its creative décor, open kitchen and sophisticated fare, Chive Blossom constantly draws a crowd. Starters on the eclectic menu range from shrimp-stuffed Medjool dates to crab nachos. Entrées lean toward seafood—don't miss the she-crab soup.

The Library – *6133 N. Kings Hwy., Myrtle Beach -* ☎*843-448-4527 - www.thelibraryrestaurantsc.com - Dinner only - Closed Sun.* With its speakeasy-style lounge, tuxedoed waitstaff and traditional tableside preparations (steak Diane, flambé desserts), The Library has been the Grand Stand's special-occasion restaurant since 1974. Rack of lamb, duck à l'orange, and twin lobster tails are just a few of the tempting selections.

$25-$50

115

Bistro 217 – *10701 Ocean Hwy., Pawleys Island -* ☎*843-235-8217 - www.bistro217.com - Closed Sun.* Dine inside or out at this casual fine-dining restaurant, located off Highway 17 in a strip of upscale shops. For big appetites at lunch, the bistro burger can't be beat. For dinner, try the 217 Treasure Chest: shrimp, scallops and grouper tossed in a basil Parmesan cream sauce over fried eggplant.

Collector's Cafe – *7740 N. Kings Hwy., Myrtle Beach -* ☎*843-449-9370 - www.collectorscafeandgallery.com - Closed Sun.* Between the ambience and the cuisine, Collector's Cafe is a masterpiece. Hand-painting decorates tables and chairs, and original artwork (for sale) lines the walls. On the menu, scallop cakes are served with a lemon beurre blanc, and a seared duck

🍴

© Gwen Cannon/Michelin

Fish tacos, Bistro 217

breast comes with bacon-braised kale and cannellini bean ragout.

Frank's and Frank's Outback – *10434 Ocean Hwy., Pawleys Island -* 📞*843 237-3030 - franksandoutback.com - Dinner only - Closed Sun.* Named for the owner of a supermarket that once stood here, Frank's has been a local favorite for 30 years. Seafood shines in cornmeal-crusted grouper, while meat lovers prefer the chophouse menu.

For outdoor dining, try **Frank's Outback** *(closed Sun & Mon)*, where you can enjoy wood-fired pizzas or heartier entrées under tall oaks. In crisp weather, there are infrared heaters and an outdoor fireplace to warm you. All year-round, live music entertains on weekends.

Greg Norman's Australian Grille – *4930 Hwy. 17 N., Myrtle Beach -* 📞*843 -361-0000 - gregnormansaustralian grille.com.* For the best vantage point, ask for a table overlooking the water at this harborside grill, owned by the golfing champion from Down Under. Located at Barefoot Landing, Greg Norman's serves up something for everyone, from tuna sashimi to Black Angus prime rib.

Hook & Barrel – *48014 N. Kings Hwy., Myrtle Beach, SC -* 📞*843-839-5888 – hookandbarrellrestaurant.com - Dinner only.* From the folks that brought you Croissants Bistro comes this new eatery, where sustainably sourced seafood rules. Go for one of the house specialties (like Myrtle Beach paella for two), or customize your meal by choosing your fresh fish (selection changes daily) and your preparation (baked, grilled, pan-seared or blackened).

Lee's Inlet Kitchen – *4460 Business 17, Murrells Inlet -* 📞*843-651-2881 - www.leesinletkitchen.com - Dinner only - Closed Sun & month of Jan.* Prices have hiked up a bit since Pearl and Eford Lee started their Murrells Inlet eatery in 1948. At that time, the fried seafood platter cost $1.50. Now it's $26.95, but it still satisfies seafood lovers with a heaping plate of flounder, fantail shrimp, oysters, scallops and deviled crab.

Sea Captain's House – *3002 N. Ocean Blvd., Myrtle Beach -* 📞*843-448-8082 - www.seacaptains.com.* This nautical-themed restaurant overlooking the Atlantic has a long history as a private beach cottage. Happily, it still welcomes patrons who enjoy good food with an ocean view. Wise choices for dinner include crab cakes, the fresh catch of the day, and a 12oz rib-eye steak. A children's menu makes this an ideal spot for families.

Under $25

Croissants Bistro and Bakery - *3751 Grissom Pkwy., Myrtle Beach -* 📞*843-448-2253 - www.croissants.net - Brunch only on Sun.* Croissants makes a good place for that pre-golf breakfast, a noon break from the sun or late afternoon tapas (the bistro closes at 6pm). For lunch, try

the pimiento and fried green tomato melt or a crab cake sandwich with house-made remoulade. Then sally up to the pastry case and drool over the mouthwatering array of cakes, cookies and tortes.

LOWCOUNTRY COAST

$50-$75

Saltus River Grill – *802 Bay St., Beaufort -* 📞*843-379-3474 - www. saltusrivergrill.com - Dinner only.* This sophisticated spot overlooking the Intracoastal Waterway occupies the site of an 18C shipyard. Local shrimp and a great selection of oysters rule at the raw bar, while signatures feature the likes of caramelized sea scallops and blackened dorado. From the wood-fired grill come Delmonico steaks, Scottish salmon and Maine lobster.

$25-$50

Breakwater – *203 Carteret St., Beaufort -* 📞*843-379-0052 - breakwatersc.com - Dinner only - Closed Sun.* «Seasonal, artisanal and original» is the stated mission of chef/owners Gary Lang and Elizabeth Shaw. Accordingly, you can taste the freshness in blackened mahi with crab beurre creole, Southern fried shrimp, and a Wagyu beef pimiento cheese burger. Save room for the Southern pecan tart.

Michael Anthony's Cucina Italiana – *37 New Orleans Rd., in Orleans Plaza, Hilton Head Island -* 📞*843-785-6272 - www.michael-anthonys.com - Dinner only - Closed Sun & Mon.* Authentic

Italian food comes to Hilton Head at this popular restaurant, whose sleek dining room is done in warm wood tones and soft colors. Dig into the likes of house-made tagliatelle with meat Bolognese, and a hearty grilled veal chop with pancetta, shallots, vodka and cream. For dessert, the tiramisu classico can't be beat.

Old Oyster Factory – *101 Marshland Rd., Hilton Head Island (1mi off Mathews Dr.) -* ☎*843-681-6040 - www.oldoysterfactory.com - Dinner only.* Built on the site of one of Hilton Head's original oyster canneries, this restaurant features oysters plucked from local waters. Diners enjoy views of Broad Creek while they dig into the broiled seafood platter, piled high with local shrimp, day-boat scallops, fresh fish, and oysters. Or order any fish simply grilled with olive oil and lemon.

Red Fish – *8 Archer Rd., Hilton Head Island -* ☎*843-686-3388 - www.redfishofhiltonhead.com - No lunch Sun.* On your way into Red Fish, stop at the restaurant's wine shop and pick up a bottle to complement the Cuban- and Caribbean-inspired fare, which ranges from Cuban black bean soup to spicy Latin ribs slathered with guava-orange barbecue sauce. The real deal is the early dining menu *(daily 5-5:45pm)*: two courses plus a beverage for under $20.

Under $25

Blackstone's Cafe – *205 Scott St., Beaufort -* ☎*843-524-4330 - www.blackstonescafe.com - Breakfast & lunch daily.* This beloved breakfast and lunchtime gathering place emphasizes local seafood in its regional offerings. It's hard to top Blackstone's shrimp and grits in the morning—stone-ground white and yellow grits are the house specialty. At midday, try the homemade soups. There's patio service too.

Shrimp Shack – *1929 Sea Island Pkwy., St. Helena Island -* ☎*843-838-2962 - Lunch Mon–Sat, dinner Fri & Sat only - Closed Sun.* Locals flock to this ultra-casual waterside eatery located 15 minutes downwind of Beaufort, which has graced St. Helena Island for more than 20 years. The shrimp burger gets raves, but the crab cakes and flounder sandwiches are not far behind. Ditch that diet and go for the hushpuppies or the sweet potato fries. Cash only.

SAVANNAH

$50-$75

Alligator Soul – *114 Barnard St. -* ☎*912-232-7899 - alligatorsoul.com - Dinner only.* Lodged underground in a c.1885 grain warehouse on Telfair Square, this fine-dining restaurant earns its stripes with organic local and regional products, starting with the inspired craft cocktails and ending with house-made desserts. In between, count on the local day boat fish and grass-fed beef to satisfy your gourmet cravings.

Husk – *12 W. Oglethorpe Ave. -* ☎*912-349-2600 - husksavannah.com - Dinner only & Sun brunch.* Culinary celebrity Sean Brock opened his fourth outpost of Husk in early 2018,

a.Lure

this time in Savannah. Here the chef's celebration of Southern cooking with hyper-regional ingredients might translate to chestnut cornbread with Georgia cane butter, or Old Chester Durocabbaw pork with hearth-baked sweet potatoes.

$25-$50

a.Lure – *309 W. Congress St. - ☎912-233-2111 - aluresavannah.com - Dinner only.* At this Historic District restaurant, a Sazerac cocktail makes a traditional prelude to contemporary cuisine that pays homage to the South. Cornmeal-dusted chicken livers, Lowcountry Boil and house-smoked duck breast with ginger and garlic barbecue sauce illustrate the theme.

The Crab Shack – *40 Estill Hammock, Tybee Island - ☎912-786-9857 - thecrabshack.com.* You'll find the freshest boiled or steamed crabs, shrimp and oysters around at this bare-bones eatery, 17 miles east of Savannah on tiny Tybee Island. You have to crack the crabs yourself, so grab a roll of paper towels and pull up a bench at one of the wooden tables.

The Grey – *109 Martin Luther King Jr. Blvd. - ☎912-662-5999 - thegreyrestaurant.com - Closed Mon.* In 2014, Johno Morisano and Chef Mashama Bailey painstakingly restored a 1938 former Greyhound bus station into a stunning Art Deco-style diner. Since then, The Grey has become one of the city's hottest spots. Regional produce, seafood and meats form the base for the chef's soulful dishes, arranged on the menu by the ingredient's origin (Dirt, Water, Pasture).

Under $25

Back in the Day Bakery – *2403 Bull St. - 912-495-9292 - backintheday bakery.com. Tue-Sun 8am-4pm - Closed Sun & Mon.* Self-taught bakers and James Beard Award nominees Cheryl and Griffith Day are famed for their extraordinary biscuits. Get one filled with herbed baked eggs or house-made breakfast sausage and jam, or enjoy the flaky buttermilk biscuits plain. Lunch adds hot and cold sandwiches—but save room for the delectable baked goods.

Mrs. Wilkes Dining Room – *107 Jones St. - 912-232-5997 - www. mrswilkes.com - Mon-Fri 11am-2pm - Closed weekends & Jan.* Folks form a line outside this Savannah institution, which was established in 1943 as a boardinghouse. Though you can no longer stay here, you can chow down on good home-style Southern food, served family-style at long communal tables.

Vinnie Van Go-Go's – *317 W. Bryan St., on Franklin Square - 912-233-6394 - www.vinnievangogo.com - No lunch Mon–Thu.* It's not fancy, but locals and visitors alike crowd the indoor and outdoor tables at Vinnie's boisterous City Market location for tasty thin-crust Neapolitan pizza. Before you come, note that Vinnie's doesn't accept credit cards or reservations.

GEORGIA'S SEA ISLANDS

Over $75

Georgian Room – *100 Cloister Dr., Sea Island, GA - 888-732-4752 - seaisland.com. Dinner only - Closed Sun & Mon.* Jackets are required for men at this elegant dining room at The Cloister. The Georgian Room fashions a posh platform with crystal chandeliers, coffered ceilings, and hand-painted china. Guests can order from the à la carte menu, which features vegan and vegetarian options, or savor the six-course chef's tasting menu.

$25-$50

Georgia Sea Grill – *407 Mallery St., St. Simons Island, GA - 912-638-1197 - georgiaseagrill.com - Dinner only - Closed Sun in winter.* Local, regional and sustainable ingredients shine at this locally owned restaurant in Pier Village. Order the fresh catch of the day prepared as you like it (with Cajun spice, bronzed, or pan-roasted) and come for discounted the First Call menu, available daily from 5pm-6.30pm at the main bar and the wine bar.

Halyard's – *58 Cinema Lane, St. Simons Island, GA - 912-638-9100 - www.halyardsrestaurant.com - Dinner only - Closed Sun.* Everything at this nautically themed fine-dining restaurant is made from scratch, from the soups and sauces to the desserts, using ingredients from area farms and purveyors. Small plates share the menu with daily specials and the day's catch—think wild Georgia shrimp, red snapper and black grouper—from local waters.

120

Where to drink

Charleston's liquid assets range from coffee shops, where superlative beans are sourced from around the globe, to urban rooftop watering holes. When you want ocean breezes and Atlantic views, head to the area's beachfront bars.

COFFEE SHOPS

1 Black Tap Coffee – **E6** – *70 ½ Beaufain St., Historic District - ☏843-793-4402 - www.blacktap coffee.com.* Baristas hand-pour each cup at the light-filled shop, where the owners globally source their beans and roast them on nearby James Island. Given Charleston's steamy weather, iced coffees are a specialty here.

2 City Lights Coffee – **E6** – *141 Market St., Historic District - ☏843 -853-7067 - www.citylightscoffee.com* Tucked away on Market Street, this cozy coffeeshop spots a bohemian vibe (they still do jam sessions) along with no-frills Counter Culture coffee (the first certified-organic coffee roaster in North Carolina)—and espresso drinks.

3 Mercantile and Mash – **E4** – *701 E Bay St., Historic District - ☏843-793-2636 – www.mercandmash.com.* Located in a renovated cigar factory, this gourmet food emporium is a great place to stop for a morning cup of joe, killer espressos, lattes made with locally sourced milk, and ample seating and on-site parking are a few more reasons to come. Every Wednesday, they offer a signature donut (flavor changes every week) made in-house.

4 The Rise Coffee Bar – **E6** – *77 Wenworth St., in The Restoration hotel, Historic District - ☏843-518-5100 - www.therestorationhotel.com.* Single-origin small-batch coffee and artisanal tea blends will start your morning off in style. Try the signature seasonal coffee, which changes throughout the year.

URBAN BARS

5 The Alley – **D4** – *131 Columbus St., Upper King - ☏843-818-4080 - www. thealleycharlestoncom.* A bowling alley and sports bar off upper King Street, The Alley has become a favorite nightspot. Eight bowling lanes, arcade games, ping pong, plus local craft beer and gourmet snack food are just a few of the reasons locals love it.

6 The Bar at Husk - **E6** – *76 Queen St., Historic District - ☏843-577-2500 - huskrestaurant.com.* Clad in century-old exposed brick, this freestanding bar located next door to Husk restaurant is a destination in itself. The bar boasts master mixologists who can whip up any libation you fancy, from pre-Prohibition to contemporary. Bourbon lovers will go gaga over the exhaustive list of Kentucky bourbons, organized by town of origin. A selection of Madeira speaks to the resurgence of fortified Portuguese wine, which was all the rage in colonial Charleston.

7 Bar Mash – *E4* – *701 E. Bay St., Historic District* - ☎*843-793-2636* - *www.barmashchs.com.* This cozy whiskey bar tucked behind Mercantile and Mash offers seasonal cocktails and a list of some 120 American whiskeys, along with entertainment such as shuffleboard, bocce, '80s arcade games, and an old-fashioned jukebox.

8 The Belmont – *D5* – *511 King St., Upper King* - ☎*843-743-3880* - *www.thebelmontcharleston.com.* Opened in 2010, The Belmont is the kind of place where black-and-white classic films play on mute and the bartender remembers regulars' favorite pours. Only 40 people at a time are allowed inside the intimate tavern.

9 Bin 152 – *E6* – *152 King St., Historic District.* ☎*843-577-7359* - *www.bin152.com.* Antiques and eye-catching art fill the walls at this cool little wine bar a block from Broad Street, where you can choose among 40 different wines by the glass and 200 by the bottle.

10 Cane Rhum Bar – *251 E. Bay St., Historic District* - ☎*843-277-2764* - *eatdrinkcane.com.* Looking for a rum drink with island ambience? At Cane Rhum Bar, cocktails like the Instant Vacation (lemongrass- and ginger-infused rum, falernum, orange and lemon juice, and ginger beer) will leave you in a laid-back frame of mind.

122

11 The Cocktail Club – *D5* – *479 King St., Upper King* - ☎*843-724-9411* - *www.thecocktailclubcharleston.com.* Next door to The MacIntosh restaurant, this intimate upstairs bar touts its farm to shaker cocktails in a restored 1881 warehouse. In addition to the list of creative cocktails, there are bar bites such as bacon popcorn. Live music plays several nights a week (schedules vary).

12 Edmund's Oast – *D2* – *1081 Morrison Dr., NoMo* - ☎*843-727-1145. edmundsoast.com.* Located in the up-and-coming NoMo (North Morrison) neighborhood, Edmund's Oast takes its name from Edmund Egan, an English brewer who made beer in Charleston in the 1760s, and the European term for the kiln used to dry hops (oast). The upscale brewpub includes an on-site brewery and a carefully curated list of local, national and international craft beers. House-cured charcuterie makes a perfect accompaniment to any brew.

13 The Gin Joint – *F6* – *182 E. Bay St., Historic District* - ☎*843-577-6111* - *theginjoint.com.* Take a seat in this dark, cozy bar—or grab a table on the brick courtyard—and swill drinks like a Churchill martini or a Corpse Reviver. The concept honors cocktails of the pre-Prohibition era, so you won't find any vodka drinks here (that spirit didn't appear on the scene until after Prohibition). Come late evening, you may even run into some local chefs.

Edmund's Oast

©Edmund's Oast/Home Team PR

123

14 The Living Room at The Dewberry – *E6* – *334 Meeting St., Historic District.* ☏*843-558-8000 - www.thedewberrycharleston.com.* Taking the place of a traditional lobby at Charleston's new ultra-chic hotel, this stunning space with its gleaming brass bar and mid-century modern décor has become one of the city's top spots to socialize and sip a cocktail.

15 Mira Winery – *E6* – *68 1/2 Queen St., Historic District* - ☏*843-722-9670 - www.miranapa.com/napa-valley-education-center-tasting-room - Open daily noon-7pm - Tastings range from $35–$65/person.* A partnership between Charleston entrepreneur Jim Dyke, Jr. and Napa Valley winemaker Gustavo Gonzalez, Mira Winery is based in the Napa Valley. Mira's Education Center is Charleston's only winery tasting room, where you can sample Mira's excellent wines and hear about the soil, topography and production process that defines these wines.

16 Prohibition – *D4* – *547 King St., Upper King* - ☏*843-793-2964 - prohibitioncharleston.com.* A 1920's speakeasy ambience infuses this bar—no secret knock required—with its bourbon-barrel ceiling and vintage décor. In addition to killer cocktails and a voluminous whiskey list, Prohibition offers live music six nights a week.

17 Proof Bar – *D5* – *437 King St., Upper King -* ℘*843-793-1422 - www. charlestonproof.com.*There are more than 30 creative cocktails to choose from at this tiny candlelit bar, but if you can't make up your mind, tell the mixologists your taste preferences and leave the libations to them.

ROOFTOP BARS

18 The Citrus Club – *E5* – *334 Meeting St, in Dewberry hotel, Historic District –* ℘*843-558-8000 - www. thedewberrycharleston.com.* There may be no better public rooftop view in the city than the breathtaking panorama from the rooftop bar at The Dewberry. Flanking the small restaurant/bar in the middle of the space, the deck wraps around for a 360-degree look over the peninsula.

19 Elevé Restaurant & Rooftop – *E6* – *55 Wentworth St., in the Grand Bohemian Hotel, Historic District -* ℘*843-724-4144 - www.grand bohemiancharleston.com.* French aperitifs such as a Kir Royale and a glass of Pernod pair well with the French-inspired menu and the view of Charleston's Historic District from the funky rooftop bar at the Grand Bohemian hotel.

20 Pavilion Bar – *E6* – *Top floor of the Market Pavilion Hotel, 225 E. Bay St., at Market St., Historic District -* ℘*843-723-0500 - www.marketpavilion.com.* Charleston harbor and the Historic District's rooftops stretch out below you at this chic city hot spot. Go before dinner to sip a cocktail and watch the sunset, or stop by for a nightcap and dessert.

21 The Rooftop Bar at Vendue – *F6* – *Top floor of The Vendue inn, 19 Vendue Range, Historic District -* ℘*843-577-7970 - www.thevendue.com.* A recent facelift has revamped Charleston's original rooftop bar, which still offers great views along with specialty cocktails, small plates and live entertainment.

22 Stars Rooftop – *D5* – *Top floor of Stars Restaurant, 495 King St., Upper King -* ℘*843-577-0100 - starsrestaurant.com.* Take in the panorama of Charleston from atop Stars Restaurant on upper King Street. International wines, specialty cocktails and craft beers make pleasant sipping while you lounge in recycled wicker chairs.

© Stars Rooftop

Stars Rooftop

23 *High Wire Distilling Co.* - *D4*

652 King St., Upper King - ☎843-755-4664.highwiredistilling.squarespace.com. High Wire takes advantage of the south's vibrant produce to hand-craft the likes of Southern Revival Jimmy Red Straight Bourbon Whiskey, which owner/distiller Scott Blackwell makes from an heirloom variety of moonshiner's corn. The centerpiece of the facility, located in a former warehouse on the far end of upper King Street, is a 530-gallon, hand-built copper still from Germany. Tours (Tue-Sat 11am-6pm, $10; must be age 21 or older) include half-ounce samples and cocktail options.

BEACH BARS

Banana Cabana
1130 Ocean Blvd., Isle of Palms - ☎843-886-4360 - www.thebanana cabanasc.com. An outdoor deck with ocean views, a sand volleyball court and a band on summer weekends make eating—and playing—here a blast.

Coconut Joe's Beach Grill and Bar
1120 Ocean Blvd., Isle of Palms - ☎843-886-0046 - www.coconutjoes.biz. Coconut Joe's beachfront upper deck is as close as you can get to the sand without being on it. Come for drink specials every day and live entertainment nightly in season.

Poe's Tavern
2210 Middle St., Sullivans Island - ☎843-883-0083 - www.poestavern. com. This popular island tavern two blocks from the beach pays homage to author Edgar Allan Poe, who was stationed at nearby Fort Moultrie for 13 months, beginning in late 1827. Poe's is the place for a late-night burger and a beer on Sullivans Island.

Rita's Seaside Grille
2 Center St., Folly Beach - ☎843-588-2525 - www.ritasseasidegrille.com. Owned by the Hall family (of Hall's Chophouse in Charleston), Rita's is the place to kick back at day's end with a plate of blackened tuna nachos and a watermelon Margarita. Live music nightly draws a young beach crowd.

The Windjammer
1008 Ocean Blvd., Isle of Palms - ☎843-886-8948 - www.the-wind jammer.com. This is the spot for bikini bashes, volleyball tournaments, bands and lots of beer. Live bands entertain here year-round on weekends.

Shopping

No wonder pirates loved this place! All the cultural delights and Southern luxuries of Charleston are enough to make any treasure-seeking buccaneer weigh anchor. This seaport shopping phenomenon offers a wealth of loot, from antiques and modern art to designer labels and Lowcountry foodstuffs. All the shops listed below are in the Historic District unless otherwise noted.

❶ Old City Market★★ – *E6*

Market St., between Meeting & E. Bay Sts. - ☏843-937-0920 - www.thecharlestoncitymarket.com - Open year-round daily - Closed Dec 25.
A three-block-long row of vendors' sheds, the historic market stretches from Meeting Street to the river along Market Street, with the newer air-conditioned **Great Hall** in the middle. The first market on this site (c.1840) was a meat market. Laws at the time required vendors to sell only fresh produce. At the end of the day, merchants threw any leftover meat into the streets, where it was devoured by vultures. Known as «Charleston eagles,» vultures were so important for this purpose that they were protected by law.

Every morning now, stalls fill with vendors peddling an array of wares, including foodstuffs, sweetgrass baskets, jewelry, beach attire, handbags and crafts.

The adjacent blocks of **Market Street** overflow with stores selling resort wear, souvenirs, and gifts.

King Street★

Charleston's major commercial thoroughfare since colonial days, King Street brims with shops, inns and restaurants. Chain stores like Talbots, J. Crew, and L'Occitane put a modern face on shopping, while connoisseurs of all things vintage will delight in poking through the antique shops along King Street between Market and Broad streets.
Once a run-down area with nary a place to eat or shop, **upper King Street** *(west of Calhoun St.)* has been revitalized with an array of trendy options. Browse through furniture, clothing and specialty stores here, along with chic art galleries and some of the city's hottest tables.

❷ Billy Reid – *E6* – 150 King St. -
☏843-577-3004 - www.billyreid.com. Award-winning Louisiana-born designer Billy Reid opened the Charleston store in 2008. Come here to ogle and purchase his latest menswear designs.

❸ Blue Bicycle Books – *E5* – 420
King St., Upper King - ☏843-722-2666 - bluebicyclebooks.com. Owned by local writer Jonathan Sanchez, Blue Bicycle carries modern first editions of Southern classics signed by the author, as well as an impressive selection of Charleston-related books.

Old City Market

4 Christian Michi – *E6* – *220 King St., at Market St.* - ☎*843-723-0575* - *www.facebook.com/christianmichisc.* Though designer ladies' clothing hangs in the window of this tony shop, inside you'll also find fine linens, colorful glassware and tableware, and chic home accessories.

5 Croghan's Jewel Box – *E6* – *308 King St.* - ☎*843-723-3594* - *www.croghansjewelbox.com.* Any Charlestonian worth his or her salt knows this revered family-run jeweler, famed for its silver, which comes in all shapes and sizes.

6 Felice Designs – *E5* – *424 King St., Upper King* - ☎*843-853-3354* - *www. felicedesigns.com.* Designer Felice Killian works jewelry magic in her creative baubles with glass beads in every color and combination.

7 George C. Birlant & Co. – *E6* – *191 King St.* - ☎*843-722-3842* - *www. birlant.com.* Established in 1922, this antique shops sparkles with crystal chandeliers and silver tea sets. Birlant is a direct importer of 18C and 19C English furniture.

8 Hamden Clothing – *E6* – *314 King St.* - ☎*843-724-6373* - *hamdenclothing.com.* This edgy downtown boutique carries styles by 60 American and European ready-to-wear and accessory brands.

9 Palm Avenue – *E6* – *251 King St.* - ☎*843-577-5219* - *shoppalmavenue. com.* Bloom in bright summer colors and flower prints by Lilly Pulitzer.

🛍

10 Savannah Bee Co. – *E6* – *270 King St.* - *☎843-722-5664. www. savannahbee.com.* Make a beeline for this retail shop to do a comparative honey tasting and purchase honey-related gifts.

11 The Shops at Belmond Charleston Place – *E6* – *King St. at Market St., in the Belmond Charleston Place hotel* - *☎843-722-4900* - *www. belmond.com.* From Tommy Bahama to Kate Spade New York, the mini mall in Charleston Place lays out a litany of classy shops.

12 Vom Fass – *E5* – *342 King St.* - *☎843-212-5714* - *charleston. vomfassusa.com.* The name is German for «from the cask», which refers to the casks on the walls that hold European-made vinegars and oils. Sample to your heart's delight, then check out the other side of the store for hand-crafted spirits.

13 West Elm – *484 King St., Upper King* – *☎843-720-3580* - *www. westelm.com.* This upscale retail chain now has a store on King Street, where, among the lovely home décor and accessories, you'll find products made by local Charleston artisans.

14 Yves Delorme – *E6* – *197 King St.* - *☎843-853-4331* - *usa.yvesdelorme. com.* Lovers of luxurious linens will drool over the pricey sheets and towels imported from France by Yves Delorme.

Art Galleries

Fine art galleries abound along East Bay Street from the Old City Market to Broad. For a lineup of galleries all in one place, check out **Gallery Row** on Broad Street *(between E. Bay &*

Meeting Sts.; charlestongalleryrow. com). Come for the **First Friday on Broad Gallery Stroll** *(first Fri of every month, 5pm-8pm)* to meet the artists and watch them work.

Here are a few gallery suggestions:

15 Anglin Smith Fine Art - *E6* - *9 Queen St.* - *☎843-853-0708* - *anglinsmith.com.*

16 Dog & Horse Fine Art - *E7* - *102 Church St.* - *☎843-577-5500* - *www.dogandhorsefineart.com.*

17 Edward Dare Gallery- *E7* - *31 Broad St.* - *☎843-853-5002* - *www.edwarddare.com.*

18 Gordon Wheeler Gallery- *F6* - *180 E. Bay St.* - *☎843-722-2546* - *www.gordonwheelergallery.com.*

19 Lowcountry Artists, Ltd. - *F6* - *148 E. Bay St.* - *☎843-577-9295* - *lowcountryartists.com.*

20 Mary Martin Gallery - *E7* - *103 Broad St.* - *☎843-640-3324* - *marymartinart.com.*

More Places to Shop
Put these on your shopping list for yourself or the folks back home.

21 Charleston Crafts Cooperative – *E6* - *161 Church St.* - *☎843-723-2938* - *www.charlestoncrafts.org.* Charleston's oldest juried craft co-op is a great place to buy sweetgrass baskets and creations in media from art glass to hand-dyed fabric—all made by South Carolina artisans.

22 Charleston Farmers' Market – *E5* - *On Marion Square, King & Calhoun Sts.* - *www.charlestonfarmersmarket. com* - *mid-Apr–Nov Sat 8am-2pm* - *Holiday Market in Dec Sat-Sun*

128

Sweetgrass Baskets

As you stroll through the Old City Market and along the streets in Charleston, or drive north on US-17 past Mt. Pleasant, you'll see women making and selling a variety of coiled grass baskets. The coiled basketry craft came to South Carolina with slaves from West Africa 300 years ago.

During the pre-Civil War plantation era, slaves winnowed rice and stored food in baskets made by coiling marsh grass with strips of palmetto leaves. In the early 20C, women began producing and selling «show baskets» made of sweetgrass, a now-scarce dune grass found along the South Carolina coast. This art form, passed down from generation to generation, is now prized as a dying folk art. Labor-intensive sweetgrass baskets take anywhere from 12 hours to 3 months to make, a fact that adds to their value as well as to their price.

9am-3pm. Tomatoes from Wadmalaw Island, okra, figs, butter beans and peaches make this market a vibrant patchwork of flavors and aromas. More than 100 vendors include farmers, growers, food purveyors and craft artisans.

㉓ Shops of Historic Charleston Foundation – *E6* - 108 Meeting St. - ☎843-724-8484 - www.historic charleston.org. Find books about Charleston (pick up a copy of the *Historic District Walking Tour* booklet) along with pewter julep cups, Charleston rice spoons, and licensed replicas of period reproduction furniture.

Must-have Souvenirs

Put these on your shopping list for yourself or the folks back home.

Sweetgrass baskets – A traditional West African art form that's survived for centuries, these woven wonders are handmade in traditional and modern forms.

Joggling boards (🕒see p. 16) – Since the early 1800s, these locally made benches have offered hours of bouncy fun.

Benne Seed Wafers
Tasty benne crackers, made from the "good luck" plant (benne is the African name for sesame seeds) that slaves brought to the Lowcountry.

Charleston Rice Spoons
These traditional long-handled silver spoons have been used to serve rice since the 18C on every «proper» Charleston table.

129

Nightlife

Think Charleston is just a place for beach parties and shoreline strolls? Think again. This coastal beacon attracts an international crowd when it comes to performing arts. With such an impressive fleet of dance, theater, and music offerings, Charleston is worth its salt as a destination for must-see productions.

HISTORIC DISTRICT

Spoleto Festival USA★★

Held in various venues in Charleston, late May–mid-June - Festival information: ☎843-722-2764 - Tickets: ☎843-579-3100 - spoletousa.org. Every spring, Italian flair meets Southern hospitality at this renowned festival. Founded in 1977 by Pulitzer prize-winning composer Gian Carlo Menotti as the counterpart to his Festival of Two Worlds in Spoleto, Italy, the arts extravaganza showcases the best of Charleston—with its intimate size and grand spaces—as a setting for more than 120 performances. Yo-Yo Ma, Emanuel Ax, the Emerson String Quartet, and Philip Glass have all appeared in years past—and the list goes on and on.

A kaleidoscope of artistic genius, the Spoleto festival includes an entire spectrum of international talent spanning opera, jazz, visual arts and multimedia presentations, to name a few. From the downtown hustle and bustle, to City Hall and throughout historic theaters and churches, Charleston offers a diverse backdrop to the festival's delights.

❶ Dock Street Theatre★ – *E6* - *135 Church St. - Box Office: ☎843-577-7183 - www.charlestonstage.com/ dock-street-theatre.html.* Concerts, operas, and plays entertain in this Historic District venue, built as a hotel in 1809 and reopened in March 2010 after undergoing a $19-million overhaul. Dock Street Theatre is home to **Charleston Stage Company,** South Carolina's largest stage troupe, which combines local talent with visiting actors to produce shows like *Beneath the Sweetgrass Moon, Ain't Misbehavin',* and *Shakespeare in Love.* The 462-seat theater boasts a wrought-iron, New Orleans-style exterior balcony and a rich interior with black-cypress wall paneling and the carved wood bas-relief of the Royal Arms of England.

Piccolo Spoleto★

Held in various venues in Charleston, late May-early June - Festival information: ☎843-724-7305 - Tickets: ☎866-811-4111 - www. piccolospoleto.com. Launched in 1979 by former mayor Joseph P. Riley, the little (or *piccolo* in Italian) sister of Spoleto, spolights local and regional creativity through poetry readings, ethnic cultural presentations, children's activities, and choral music. Highlights from previous festivals include outdoor juried art exhibitions,

Courtesy of Charleston Stage

Dock Street Theatre

public art projects, music block parties, and improvisational comedy. Venues range from the commonplace (Starbucks) to the sublime (the French Huguenot Church).

Charleston Symphony Orchestra
☏843-723-7528 - Tickets: ☏843-242-3099 - www.charlestonsymphony.com
Formed in 1918 as a loosely organized group that played mainly for friends, the Charleston Symphony Orchestra held its first formal concert in 1936 in Hibernian Hall. The professional symphony that now exists dates to 1970, when the group performed Charleston's first production of George Gershwin's folk opera *Porgy and Bess,* based on the novel by native son Dubose Heyward.

Today, a resplendent cast of musicians and guest artists (Itzhak Perlman, Pinchas Zukerman, Marvin Hamlisch, Judy Collins) fill every season *(Sept-Apr)* with sweeping sound and artistry. The CSO has recently performed at a variety of venues, but the new **Gaillard Center**, opened in fall 2015, now serves as the Symphony's home stage. The group, which includes 30 professional full-time musicians, brings the joy of music to the masses through a regular schedule of community concerts, school programs, and their major concert series: Masterworks, the Charleston Pops and the Chamber Orchestra.

✕ ADDRESSES

Theater 411

For the latest on what's playing in Charleston, check out Theatre Charleston, a nonprofit alliance whose members consist of the area's leading local theaters. Their calendar will fill you in on all the theatrical happenings while you're in town: theatrecharleston.com.

② Gaillard Center – *E5* -
95 Calhoun St. - ☏843-242-3099 - www.gaillardcenter.com. Reopened in October 2015 after a $142 million renovation, this 1968 performance venue has been reimagined as the gleaming white, Neoclassical Gaillard Center. Named for J. Palmer Gaillard (mayor of the city from 1959-75), the venue was designed by David M. Schwarz Architects of Washington, DC,

132

Sottile Theatre College of Charleston

in the grand style of Europe's great opera houses. The 1,800-seat Performance Hall boasts superb acoustics, three tiers of balconies and a gorgeous dome overhead. A world-class venue, The Gaillard Center hosts the Charleston Symphony Orchestra and Spoleto USA performances as well as a mix of genres from rock and hip- hop concerts to classical ballet and Broadway musicals.

③ Footlight Players – *E6* –
20 Queen St. - ☏843-722-4487 - www.footlightplayers.net. They aren't called «footlight» for nothing—this company has relocated more than three times since their inception in 1931, temporarily occupying the Navy Yard and Dock Street Theatre at different times over the years.

Today the Players' performance venue resides in a large, renovated cotton warehouse on Queen Street, making the most of the company's long-standing tradition to deliver top-notch performances including musicals, love stories and dramas.

④ The Have Nots! – *E5* – *Theatre 99 at 280 Meeting St. - ☏843-853-6687 - theatre99.com.* Charleston may seem to be the epitome of etiquette, but this multifaceted city also holds its own in uproarious antics. If you want to wear yourself

© Gwen Cannon/Michelin

out with laughter, look no farther than this hilarious improv troupe, which performs at Theatre 99. Along the lines of Chicago's famed Second City, the humor of these quick-witted actors keeps audiences howling at interactive skits and ingenious spontaneity.

5 Sottile Theatre College of Charleston – *E5* – *44 George St., on the College of Charleston campus - ℘843-953-6340 - sottile.cofc.edu.* If you wish upon a star, you might end up in this twinkling theater on the College of Charleston campus, with its trademark saucer-shaped dome. Look up to marvel at the blue expanse of ceiling, accented with a sprinkling of tiny lights. Built in 1922 by entertainment entrepreneur Albert Sottile, the theater hosted films and vaudeville productions. A meticulous structural renovation in 1986 updated the theater's nuts and bolts, and added a spacious lobby. Further renovations in 2011 uncovered the remnants of original murals painted in the 1920s. With all its improvements, the 785-seat theater continues to welcome an outstanding lineup of shows, including those from the Spoleto USA Festival.

UPPER KING STREET

6 Music Farm- *E5* - *32 Ann St., Upper King - ℘843-577-6989 - www.musicfarm.com.* This renovated storage depot is one of the hippest barns around, but the VIPs aren't your average livestock. Instead, the spacious, multilevel space welcomes music lovers and musicians from near and far. Tones of simplicity, from original brickwork to exposed beams, keep the focus on the music, while the jazzy mezzanines keep it fresh. Previous performers include national acts such as Edwin McCain, They Might Be Giants, and Sheryl Crow, but The Farm stages some of the best local bands as well.

7 Woolfe Street Playhouse – *D4* - *34 Woolfe St. - ℘843-856-1579 - woolfestreetplayhouse.com.* Recently transformed into a 200-seat performance space, this former meat-packing warehouse (built in 1914) in the upper King Street corridor is now home to the **Village Repertory Company**. The professional, nonprofit theater company stages drama, comedy and musicals, emphasizing lesser-known classics and new works.

NORTH CHARLESTON

North Charleston Coliseum & Performing Arts Center
5001 Coliseum Dr., North Charleston - ℘843-529-5000. Tickets: ℘800-745-3000 - www.northcharleston coliseumpac.com. This oval arena takes on many shapes during the year. The 13,000-seat facility stages everything from sporting events—it's the home court of the South Carolina Stingrays East Coast Hockey League team—to energetic Broadway productions, as well as concert performances by the North Charleston Pops.

Where to stay

High season in Charleston and Savannah is in the spring and fall. Hotel rates are considerably lower during the hot, humid summer and the mild winter months. High season for the resort islands is in summer.

The properties listed below were selected for their ambience, location and/or value for money. Prices reflect the average cost for a standard double room for two people in high season. Price ranges quoted do not reflect any resort fees or the Charleston, SC, hotel tax rate of 13.5%.

Locate the addresses on the detachable plan using the numbered pads (ex. ①). The coordinates in red (ex. D2) refer to the same plan.

134

CHARLESTON HISTORIC DISTRICT

Over $500

① Belmond Charleston Place – *E6* *205 Meeting St. (main entrance off Hassell St.) - ☎843-722-4900 or ☎888-635-2350 - www.belmond. com/charleston-place - wfi - 435 rooms.* A 3,000-piece Murano crystal chandelier hangs above the Georgian open-armed staircase in the lobby of the grand dame of Charleston's lodgings. Newly renovated guest rooms have 19C period furnishings, master-controlled lighting, and sumptuous marble baths. Rooms on the Club Level offer private concierge service, plus breakfast, cocktails and hors d'oeuvres in the Club Lounge. Amenities include a spa, indoor pool, fitness center and adjoining shops. Be sure to savor the innovative cuisine at the hotel's renowned **Charleston Grill**.

② Market Pavilion Hotel – *F6* *225 E. Bay St. - ☎843-723-0500- www.marketpavilion.com - wifi - 70 rooms.* This luxury property enjoys a great location on the busy corner of East Bay and Market streets. Your room will have its own foyer, mahogany furnishings and double-paned windows. Sleep in style on Frette linens, with cashmere blankets and down pillows. Italian marble baths come with fluffy towels and robes. Off the lobby, **Grill 225** specializes in chophouse fare, while the rooftop **Pavilion Bar** boasts a harbor view.

③ Zero George – *E5* – *0 George St. - ☎843-817-7900 or ☎855-242-1864 - zerogeorgecom - wifi - 16 rooms.* Set around a charming brick courtyard, five early-19C houses offer luxurious rooms and suites that retain original architectural elements such as heart pine floors, high ceilings and period millwork. A European continental buffet, included in the rate, is set up each morning in the bar. Guests can enjoy breakfast in the cozy dining room or outside in the palmetto-shaded courtyard before taking complimentary bikes to explore the Historic District.

$350-$500

④ Andrew Pinckney Inn – *E6*
– *40 Pinckney St. ☏843-937-8800 or ☏800-505-8983 - andrewpinckneyinn.com - wifi - 41 rooms.* This inn is well situated two blocks from the Old City Market. The original 1840 structure was renovated in 2001, at which time the inn added six rooms and three townhouse suites in a new building across the street. Enjoy a complimentary breakfast, and, in season, a welcome reception on the rooftop terrace while you scope out the sights of the city.

⑤ Grand Bohemian Hotel – *E6*
55 Wentworth St. - ☏843-722-5711 or ☏888-472-6312 - www.grand bohemiancharleston.com - wifi - 50 rooms. The first of the sumptuous Kessler Collection properties in Charleston, the Grand Bohemian opened in summer 2015. Fine art is displayed in the public spaces and French-accented rooms of this upscale art-centric hotel. A wine blending and tasting room caters to oenophiles, while a fitness center occupies the active set. Rooftop **Éleve** restaurant serves modern American cuisine.

⑥ Harbour View Inn – *F6* – *2 Vendue Range - ☏843-853-8439 or ☏888-853-8439 - harbourviewcharleston. com - wifi - 52 rooms.* Adjacent to Waterfront Park, this family-friendly property overlooks Charleston Harbor. The lobby décor recalls the days when many of Charleston's residents hailed from the Caribbean. Lowcountry-style guest rooms feature 14-foot ceilings, four-poster beds and wicker furniture. Rates include a continental breakfast, an evening wine and cheese reception, cookies and milk before bedtime, and evening turn-down service.

⑦ Mills House Hotel – *E6* – *115 Meeting St. - ☏843-577-2400 or ☏800-874-9600 - www.millshouse. com - wifi - 216 rooms.* This Wyndham Grand hotel has nearly everything you could ask for in a moderately priced property: an outdoor pool, a courtyard, two bars, the **Barbadoes Room** restaurant (try their Sunday brunch) and a Grand Ballroom. Well-appointed rooms boast period furnishings and come with nightly turn-down service. The three popular poolside rooms all have private porches on the second-floor sun deck.

⑧ Planters Inn – *E6* – *112 N. Market St. - ☏843-722-2345 or ☏800-845-7082 - www.plantersinn.com - wifi - 64 rooms.* This Relais & Châteaux property occupies the corner of Market and Meeting streets in the historic district. Lodgings in the original 1844 building are designed in subtle colors with four-poster canopy beds, reproduction pieces and high ceilings. The piazza building features 21 newly renovated Charleston Garden Courtyard Suites overlooking the stunning, palm-studded courtyard from a breezy loggia. Sample contemporary American fare at the inn's romantic **Peninsula Grill**.

⑨ Wentworth Mansion – *D6*
– *149 Wentworth St. - ☏843-853-1886 or ☏888-466-1886 - www. wentworthmansion.com - wifi - 21 rooms.* Five blocks off King Street, Wentworth Mansion envelops guests

in opulent surroundings with and-carved marble fireplaces and Tiffany stained-glass windows in spacious quarters built for a wealthy cotton merchant in 1886. Begin the day with a complimentary breakfast buffet on the sunporch, and end it with contemporary fare at the on-site **Circa 1886** restaurant.

$200-$350

10 **The Dewberry** – *E5* – *334 Meeting St.* - *☎843-558-8000 - www.thedewberrycharleston.com - wifi - 254 rooms.* Developer John Dewberry gutted and reimagined this 1964 federal office building as an elegant hotel. Mid-century modern furnishings adorn the **Living Room**, highlighted by a gleaming brass bar. Once in your room, stow your belongings in the wardrobe faced with hand-painted wallpaper and curl up in Irish linen bedding. **Henrietta's**, off the lobby, does French brasserie fare with panache. And don't miss the rooftop **Citrus Club**, with its unparalled view of the city.

11 **Francis Marion Hotel** – *E5* – *387 King St.* - *☎843-722-0600 or ☎877-756-2121 - francismarion hotel.com - wifi - 234 rooms.* Named for Revolutionary War hero Francis Marion (aka the «Swamp Fox»), this hotel premiered in 1924 at the corner of Calhoun and King streets, near shopping, restaurants, and the College of Charleston. Restored in 1996, the 12-story hotel encloses rooms with high ceilings and European style coupled with modern amenities. Downstairs is the inviting **Spa Adagio**.

12 **French Quarter Inn** – *E6* – *166 Church St.* - *☎843-722-1900 or ☎866-812-1900 - fqicharleston.com - wifi - 50 rooms.* Guests are greeted with a glass of Champagne at check-in in the elegant lobby of this hotel, located just around the corner from Market Street. At night, enjoy milk and cookies before slipping into the triple-sheeted European bedding and choose one of seven different selections from the pillow menu. Service is a cut above, and Parisian charm outfits rooms with carved headboards and toile bed throws. The adjoining **Ruth's Chris Steak House** specializes in aged USDA Prime Midwestern beef.

13 **Fulton Lane Inn** – *E6* – *202 King St.* - *☎843-720-2600 or ☎800-720-2688 - www.fultonlaneinn.com - wifi - 45 rooms.* Since Fulton Lane Inn is hidden on a tiny lane off King Street, you'll be spared some of the noise from this busy commercial thoroughfare, yet still have easy access to great shopping right outside your door. King Deluxe rooms have four-poster canopy beds and in-room refrigerators; some even feature fireplaces and whirlpool tubs. The friendly staff is happy to help you make restaurant reservations and arrange sightseeing tours.

14 **Governor's House Inn** – *E7* – *117 Broad St.* - *☎843-720-2070 or ☎800-720-9812 - www.governors house.com - wifi - 11 rooms.* When Governor Edward Rutledge lived here in the late 1700s, this mansion, with its crystal chandeliers, nine fireplaces and double piazzas, entertained many local notables. Individually

©Gwen Cannon/Michelin

137

Francis Marion Hotel

decorated rooms are outfitted with period furnishings; many boast private porches and whirlpool baths. Amenities include free on-site parking, a continental breakfast and afternoon tea.

15 Hampton Inn Historic District – *E5* - 345 Meeting St. - ☎843-723-4000 or ☎800-426-7866 - *www.hamptoninn.com* - wifi - 171 rooms. Adjacent to the Charleston Visitor Center, this former 19C railroad warehouse now welcomes guests as a Hampton Inn. Clean, comfortable rooms sport an antebellum décor, with mahogany furnishings and floral prints. The hotel offers a pool and fitness center and a complimentary hot breakfast, also avaliable to go.

16 Indigo Inn – *E6* – 1 Maiden Lane - ☎843-577-5900 or ☎800-845-7639 - *www.indigoinn.com* - wifi - 40 rooms. Built in the mid-19C as a warehouse to store indigo (a plant used to make blue dye), this building was converted into a bed-and-breakfast in 1979. A block away from the Old City Market, the Indigo lodges guests in rooms—most overlooking the courtyard—outfitted with Colonial-style furnishings. In the morning, guests can enjoy the complimentary breakfast inside or in the lovely courtyard.

17 John Rutledge House Inn – *E7* – 116 Broad St. - ☎843-723-7999 or ☎800-476-9741 - *www.johnrutledge houseinn.com* - wifi - 19 rooms.

A rough draft of the Constitution was written in this 1763 house, and resident John Rutledge was one of the 55 men who signed it. Inlaid parquet floors, canopied rice beds, carved plaster moldings, antiques and period reproductions typify this National Historic Landmark's restoration to its mid-18C appearance. A continental breakfast and evening libations are complementary.

18 **Two Meeting Street Inn** – *E7 – 2 Meeting St. - ☎843-723-7322 or ☎888-723-7322 - www. twomeetingstreet.com - wifi - 9 rooms.* At the tip of The Battery, this 19C home overlooking the water is known for gracious hospitality. The Queen Anne Victorian was built for newlyweds Waring and Martha Carrington in 1890. Inside, English oak woodwork, Tiffany stained-glass windows and crystal chandeliers bespeak the means of the wealthy couple. Ask the concierge to make dinner reservations and arrange for sightseeing tours or theater tickets.

19 **The Vendue** – *F6 – 19 Vendue Range - ☎843-577-7970 or ☎800 845-7900 - thevendue.com - wifi - 84 rooms.* The Vendue is carved out of two 18C warehouses. A rotating art collection fills the hallway off the marble-floored lobby. Rates include a glass of bubbly upon arrival, an afternoon art reception, bedtime milk and cookies, and use of bicycles for exploring. Choose fine dining in the **Revival** restaurant or light fare and cocktails on **The Rooftop.**

138

OFF THE PENINSULA

Over $500

The Sanctuary – *1 Sanctuary Beach Dr., Kiawah Island - ☎843-768-2121 or ☎800-576-1570 - www. thesanctuary.com - wifi - 255 rooms.* Designed to resemble a 19C seaside mansion, this luxurious oceanfront resort hotel is flanked by 150-year-old transplanted live oaks. The lobby feels like someone's lavish living room, with its 25-foot-high ceilings and unobstructed ocean view. Room décor sports marsh tones of green and gold, while marble baths have deep soaking tubs. Sun yourself on the beach and the palm-studded pool deck, or luxuriate at the spa. Later, enjoy fine contemporary cuisine at the **Ocean Room**, or Lowcountry fare at casual **Jasmine Porch.**

$200-$350

The Boardwalk Inn – *200 Grand Pavilion Blvd., at Wild Dunes resort, Isle of Palms - ☎843-886-6000 or ☎888-778-1876 - www.wilddunes.com - wifi - 94 rooms.* If you don't want to rent a place for a whole week at Wild Dunes resort, this oceanfront inn is a great option. You'll still have access to all the resort's amenities, which include a fitness center, tennis courts, and two award-winning golf courses. When you're not relaxing in your balconied room, you can pedal along the bike paths, swim in the pools, or just relax on the wide white-sand beach.

The Inn at Middleton Place – *4290 Ashley River Rd., at Middleton Place Plantation - ☎843-556-0500 or ☎855-516-1090 - www.theinnat middletonplace.com - wifi - 55 rooms.* You're sure to feel close to nature at this inn, adjacent to Middleton Place. Contemporary rooms have floor-to-ceiling windows, plantation shutters, handmade furnishings and braided rugs. With the price comes a daily breakfast in the Lake House and evening wine and hors-d'oeuvres. Bicycles can be rented to explore the grounds. You'll also receive free passes to Middleton Place Gardens, the House Museum and Stableyards.

THE GRAND STRAND

$200-$350

The Breakers Resort – *2006 N. Ocean Blvd., Myrtle Beach, SC - ☎843-444-4444 or ☎855-861-9550 - www. breakers.com - wifi - 530 rooms.* The Breakers has been a Myrtle Beach landmark for 70 years. The hotel comprises three separate buildings. Standard rooms, most with balconies, are done in light woods and tropical hues. The North Tower houses one-, two- and three-room suites, and spacious condominiums, while the new Dunes building offers renovated value rooms. No matter which locale you choose, the kids will love the oceanfront water park.

Sea View Inn – *414 Myrtle Ave., Pawleys Island - ☎843-237-4253 - www.seaviewinn.com - 20 rooms.* The rambling, two-story inn sits on its own private beach. That fact, plus a friendly staff, rooms with air-conditioning and private baths, three meals a day included in the rate, and the absence of TVs and phones lure guests back year after year.

Hampton Inn Broadway at the Beach – *1140 Celebrity Circle, Myrtle Beach - ☎843-916-0600 or ☎800-426-7866 - www. hamptoninnbroadway.com - wifi - 141 rooms.* If you don't mind being off the beach, this Hampton Inn sits by the lake at the heart of the-acre entertainment complex Broadway at the Beach. Shops, restaurants, mini-golf, Ripley's Aquarium and many other amusements will be right outside your door. You'll also receive standard Hampton amenities like a complimentary hot breakfast.

BEAUFORT AREA

$350-$500

Montage Palmetto Bluff – *476 Mt. Pelia Rd., Bluffton, SC - ☎843-706-6500 or ☎866-706-6565 - www. montagehotels.com/palmettobluff - wifi - 200 rooms.* With its high-end amenities, this Montage property overlooks the May River on 20,000 acres and caters to sybarites. The property added a new inn in 2016 to complement the 50 luxe cottages with heart-pine floors, fireplaces, steam showers and screened-in porches. Savor fine Lowcountry cuisine in the newly renovated

Octagon or local seafood at the **Canoe Club**, indulge in the spa, and test your skill on the 18-hole Jack Nicklaus Signature golf course.

$200-$350

Anchorage 1770 – *1103 Bay St., Beaufort - ☏877-951-1770 - www.anchorage1770.com - wifi - 15 rooms.* This inn peers out over the Beaufort River, two blocks from the heart of Bay Street shopping and dining. True to its name, the house dates to 1770. In the early 1900s, the mansion was purchased by Admiral Lester Beardsley, who added the two upper porches and stately columns, and decorated the interior with lovely Adam-style detailing. Ask for a river-view room on the second or third floor, where you'll have access to the airy furnished porches.

SAVANNAH

$200-$350

The Brice – *5 W. Jones St., Savannah, GA - ☏912-238-1200 or ☏877-482-7423 - www.bricehotel.com - wifi - 145 rooms.* In Savannah's Historic District, a block from River Street, this boutique hotel was carved out of a c.1860s warehouse. When you're not relaxing or treating yourself to a spa service in your stylishly chic room, check out the outdoor pool or take one of the complimentary bikes for a spin.

The Gastonian – *220 E. Gaston St., Savannah. ☏912-232-2869 or ☏800-322-6603. www.gastonian.com - wifi - 17 rooms.* Attentive service defines Southern hospitality in the two adjoining Regency-style mansions that house this luxurious Historic District

140

Anchorage 1770

©Anchorage 1770

©Anchorage 1770

Jekyll Island Club Hotel

inn. All guest quarters have working fireplaces and are elegantly appointed with Oriental rugs and antique beds. For breakfast, choose from the likes of lemon ricotta pancakes, made-to-order omelets, and fresh-baked scones.

GEORGIA'S GOLDEN ISLES

$350-$500

The Cloister – *100 Salt Marsh Lane, Sea Island, GA - ☎912-638-3611 or ☎855-572-4975 - www.seaisland.com - wifi - 165 rooms.* Built in 1928 by famed Florida architect Addison Mizner, The Cloister has been gracefully renovated. Guests can choose among rooms in three distinctive buildings: the original Cloister, Beach Club suites, and Ocean villas. While the kids are busy with organized resort activities, you can relax on five miles of beach, escape to the Spa at Sea Island, play a set of tennis or hit the links. Dining at The **Georgian Room** is always a special occasion.

$200-$350

Jekyll Island Club Hotel – *371 Riverview Dr., Jekyll Island, GA - ☎912-635-2600 or ☎855-535-9547 - www.jekyllclub.com - wifi - 157 rooms.* Completed in 1888 as a hunting retreat for America's wealthy elite, this restored clubhouse, now a National Historic Landmark, retains its turn-of-the-century charm. The renovated historic Crane (1917) and Cherokee (1904) cottages offer additional rooms and suites. With 63 holes of golf, 13 clay tennis courts, and a beach club nearby (free shuttle for guests), you may never want to leave. Save a night to feast on regional cuisine in the **Grand Dining Room**.

Find Out More

Patriots Point Naval & Maritime Museum
©Patriots Point Naval & Maritime Museum

Southern Belle

Charleston was born in 1670 when a group of 150 English colonists in two ships landed on high ground along the western bank of the Ashley River. They named their settlement Charles Towne (after King Charles II), and set about building a fort to keep the colonists safe from the Spanish. Settlers slept within the fortified walls at night. During the day, they worked the fields where they grew crops such as oranges, lemons, limes, pomegranates, figs, wheat, potatoes, and flax.

By 1672, Charles Towne boasted 30 homes and 200 people. But the swampy, mosquito-ridden settlement became so plagued by disease and hunger during its first decade that the colonists decided to move the town to a better location on the peninsula across the river. In 1680, they disembarked at a site just north of the gleaming white oyster bank (now White Point Gardens) that the original settlers had passed on their initial journey upriver.

A GRAND COLONIAL CITY

Charles Towne's new location, surrounded by the Cooper and Ashley rivers, was a natural site for trade. A plan was made for the city's layout before any structures were built. One visitor in 1682 described the nascent city as "regularly laid out into large and capacious streets, which to buildings is a great ornament and beauty."

With the influx of settlers from elsewhere in the colonies, as well as from Europe (French Huguenots, English, Irish, Scots) and Barbados, Charles Towne grew to be the fifth-largest city in colonial America, with

The End of the Lord Proprietors

When King Charles II returned from exile in 1661 to assume the English throne, he showed his gratitude to those who had been most loyal to him by naming eight Lord Proprietors and granting to them all the territory now occupied by North Carolina, South Carolina and Georgia.

The Lord Proprietors, however, took little interest in the colonies that were established on their lands. After their overseers failed to send troops to protect Charles Towne from Spanish attack, the colonists revolted. One thing led to another, and in 1721, the reign of the Lord Proprietors ended when South Carolina became a royal colony, under a British governor.

The Huguenots

*In April 1680, the ship Richmond arrived in Charleston with 45 French Protestants aboard. Called Huguenots, they were seeking to escape religious persecution under King Louis XIV in their native France. Hundreds more followed, and in 1687, they built a church on what is now the corner of Church Street and Queen Street in downtown Charleston. The current **French Huguenot Church** (1845) at 136 Church Street is the third to be erected on the site and the first Gothic Revival structure in the city. Today names such as Manigault, Ravenel, Huger and Gaillard, descendants of those early Huguenots, are woven into the fabric of Charleston's culture.*

a population of 1,200 by 1690. As the 18C dawned, Charles Towne was a prosperous colonial city, with a wealthy merchant class supporting its bustling port. Stately private homes went up, some with their own wharves. The main road out of the city was dubbed the Broad Way, and proclaimed to be beautiful and green all year. Thriving Charles Towne, the economic, social, and political center of the Lowcountry, became known as a "little London" in the New World. The charter of early Charles Towne guaranteed religious freedom, and the colony welcomed a host of worshippers, including French Huguenots and other Protestants, Jews and Catholics. Owing to its religious diversity and the number of different churches that were built on the peninsula, Charleston became known as

The Holy City, a moniker it retains to this day.

To protect its citizens from attack by the Spanish and unfriendly Indians, fortified walls made of local brick, palmetto logs and tabby were built around the city in the late 17C along the boundaries of the Cooper River and present-day Meeting Street. By 1718, however, with most of the colonists' enemies gone, the walls were taken down to make room for the expanding city.

Eventually, the wealthy merchants became successful planters, thanks to the cultivation of rice. It was the black slaves who taught the European

145

© James Schwabel / age fotostock

Antebellum houses on East Battery Street

planters how to grow rice, as they had been doing it for centuries in their homelands in Africa. Rice, along with indigo and, later, cotton thrived along the coast in the Lowcountry's temperate, humid climate. By the late 1700s, hundreds of plantations, fueled by slave laborers brought from the west coast of Africa, dotted the landscape. The wealthy planters developed into an aristocracy, leaving their disease-ridden plantations to the slaves in the sweltering summer and retiring to their city homes in Charlestown for a season of elite socializing.

WAR YEARS

In 1776, the crude palmetto rampart at Fort Moultrie on Sullivan's Island held off a British fleet of 11 ships carrying 270 guns. For the next three years, Charles Towne was spared further involvement in the Revolution. That respite would not last, however. The British attacked again in 1778, on their way north from taking Savannah, and occupied Charlestown for the remainder of the war. Two years later, in 1983, a new municipal government was formed, and the city was incorporated as Charleston.

As a consensus against slavery was building in 1858 in the northern states, Charleston held fast to an economy whose wealth was inextricably tied to slavery. In December 1860, South Carolina seceded from the Union. A week later, Major Robert Anderson moved his federal troops from Fort Moultrie to a new battlement, **Fort Sumter**, located in Charleston Harbor.

Over several months, Major Anderson refused to leave Sumter, until finally, General Beauregard gave him one last ultimatum. When Anderson still did not surrender, Confederate forces fired the first shots of the Civil War, which rang out in Charleston Harbor in the morning hours of April 12, 1861, and changed the city forever.

A high-priority target for the Union as South Carolina's second-largest port, Charleston fell under siege beginning in 1863. The lower part of the city was pummeled with incendiary bombs and shells off and on, until the end of the war.

By that time, the once-thriving port had been shelled into a virtual ghost town. One reporter who saw the city in 1865, described it as "a city of ruins, of desolation, of vacant houses, . . .of rotting wharves . . . and weed-wild gardens." As a result of the abolition of slavery and the poverty that besieged the South after the war, the region's plantation economy gradually disintegrated. Left "too poor to paint, too proud to whitewash," Charlestonians were forced to adapt, rather than remodel, their beautiful historic buildings.

AN INTREPID SPIRIT

In the mid-1920s, Charleston's antebellum mansions were crumbling and the city's economy was depressed. Enter a group of local artists and writers who sought to bring attention to the city's rich cultural heritage. Writer DuBose Heyward—who penned the 1925 book *Porgy*, on which composer George Gershwin based his

Charleston Facts

- The oldest public building in South Carolina is Charleston's Powder Magazine (see p 00), built in 1713 to store the city's supply of gunpowder.
- Dr. Alexander Garden, a Charleston physician, was the first person to import the Cape Jasmine plant from South Africa in 1754. The flower, now found in gardens throughout the city, was renamed Gardenia in his honor.
- On August 31, 1886, a 7.6-magnitude earthquake—the strongest quake ever recorded in the southeastern U.S.—rocked the city of Charleston.
- Until the early 19C, Charleston had the largest Jewish population of any city in North America.
- The Arthur Ravel Jr. Bridge—known to locals as the Cooper River Bridge—is the longest (1,546 feet) cable-stay bridge in North America.
- The Charleston RiverDogs Class A baseball team, an affiliate of the New York Yankees, actually has a Director of Fun: team co-owner and actor Bill Murray, who lives in town.

folk opera *Porgy and Bess* in 1935; and Charleston painter Elizabeth O'Neill Verner, along with others, all interpreted the Lowcountry folkways in their art. Their music, books and canvases created images of daily life in Charleston and the nearby plantations for the world to see. The cultural renewal they launched, later known as the **Charleston Renaissance**, emphasized American values and realism. The sense of civic pride it fostered would eventually fuel Charleston's historic preservation movement. Hounded by natural disasters over the years, plucky Charleston has rebuilt itself after repeated attacks of disease, fires, hurricanes and earth-quakes (the city sits on the second most active fault in the US). To protect its historic structures, Charleston became the first American city to enact a historic zoning ordinance in 1931.

Despite the ravages of the centuries, Charleston today is better than ever. Home to more than 250 tech companies, this fast-growing city handles $65 billion in imports and exports through the Port of Charleston. And that's not to mention the $37 million that the new cruise port is expected to generate annually. The arrival of Boeing in North Charleston in 2009 amounted to an investment of $2 billion in land, facilities, infrastructure and machinery at its 787 Dreamliner production plant.

Among its many accolades as a city known for its hospitality and its superlative food, Charleston is more importantly hailed as a "living museum" for its storied history and its stunning 18C and 19C **architecture★★★**.

Architecture

One of Charleston's many charms lies in its architecture. From the pastel facades of Rainbow Row to the grand antebellum mansions along The Battery, Charleston claims one of the largest collections of historic public buildings and private dwellings left in any city in the South. In fact, the entire **Historic District★★★** was designated a National Historic Landmark District in 1960.

ODE TO PRESERVATION

A stroll along The Battery and through the streets of the Historic District reveals a primer of architectural styles, beginning with Early Georgian (1700-1760), continuing through Adamesque (1790-1815), Greek Revival (1830-1875) and Italianate (1850-1885) to Queen Anne(1880-1900) and Art Deco (1910-1940).

Many homes have ornamental wrought-iron gates enclosing enchanting landscaped gardens. You'll also note a preponderance of white steeples on the city's skyline. These churches, which represent a host of different faiths, account for Charleston's moniker, the Holy City. The fact that so many of Charleston's historic structures have been preserved is a testament to organizations such as the Society for the Preservation of Old Dwellings and the Commission on Planning and Zoning, both established in the 1920s. Their work paved the way for Charleston passing America's first major preservation ordinance in 1931. The Historic Charleston Foundation followed in 1947, established as a nonprofit organization dedicated to preserving and protecting the architectural, historical and cultural character of the city and the surrounding area.

EARLY ARCHITECTS

Gabriel Manigault (1758-1809), a third-generation Charlestonian, was the city's first amateur architect. He is credited with introducing the Adamesque style to Charleston in the home he designed for his brother, the **Joseph Manigault House★** *(350 Meeting St. see p. 33).*

A Charleston native who attended the College of Charleston, **Robert Mills** (1781-1855) is the first native-born American to be trained as an architect. He is best-known for his design of the Washington Monument in Washington, DC. In Charleston, his works include the **Circular Congregational Church★★** *(150 Meeting St.)* and the Greek Doric-style Fireproof Building nearby at 100 Meeting Street.

UNIQUELY CHARLESTON

The city's most distinctive architectural style is the **Single House**. Positioned with the length

© The Charleston Museum

Joseph Manigault House **149**

of the house perpendicular to the street, the single house derives from a style imported by the Barbadians, who were among the first settlers at Charles Towne. You'll recognize a Single House by the false front door facing the street. These houses, one room wide with airy double covered piazzas (as porches are called in these parts), are positioned to catch the prevailing breezes off the water. The actual entrance is off the ground-level piazza.

Charleston's dedication to preserving its beautiful historic buildings has resulted in making the city one of America's most important architectural resources and the vibrant place it is today. Everywhere you look, the past is etched in stone.

Charleston Rocks

On 9:51pm on August 31, 1886, Charlestonians were awakened with an ominous rumbling. Within minutes, a 7.6-magnitude earthquake shook the city to its core, with a tremor that was felt as far away as Boston. The strongest quake ever recorded in the Southeastern U.S., this shaker racked up more than $5.5 million worth of damage, and was reportedly responsible for 60 deaths. As you tour the Historic District, note the small metal disks and stars on home façades. These mark earthquake rods, added to shore up structures built after the devastating quake. The rods pass through the building's joists and are connected by decorative bolts on the outer walls.

Activities for Kids

From Patriots Point to a day at the beach, kids get a kick out of Charleston. Here are a few good ways to entertain the young and the restless while you're in town.

The following sights listed within the guide are geared specifically toward children:

South Carolina Aquarium★★ - *100 Aquarium Wharf - ☎843-577-3474 - www.scaquarium.org.* Fishy fun for all ages. ♿*See p26.*

Patriot's Point Naval & Maritime Museum★★ – *40 Patriots Point Rd., Mt. Pleasant - ☎843-884-2727 - www.patriotspoint.org.* Kids love scrambling up and down the decks on the USS *Yorktown*, the centerpiece of Patriots Point. ♿*See p56.*

Children's Museum of the Lowcountry – *25 Ann St. - ☎843-853-8962 - www.explorecml.org.* Crafts, activities, and learning experiences just for kids. ♿*See p38.*

CELEBRATE THE SEASONS AT MIDDLETON PLACE

4300 Ashley River Rd. - ☎843-556-6020 - www.middletonplace.org - $28 adults (gardens & stableyards), $10 children (ages 6-13) - free for children age 5 and under. ♿*See p 46).*
Once a working plantation, **Middleton Place★★★** hosts a year-round schedule of events that capitalize on its past and appeal to the whole family. Here are a couple of our favorites.

Easter Eggstravaganza – *Easter Saturday morning - free with plantation admission.* Bring a basket to hunt for hard-boiled eggs in the Middleton Place gardens. Then take your finds to the stableyard to dye them and enjoy Colonial games, an old-fashioned egg roll, and Easter crafts.

Plantation Days – *Mid-Nov - free with Middleton Place admission.* Gullah storytelling and artisan craft demonstrations (sugarcane pressing, leather tanning) make antebellum plantation life come alive during this fall celebration.

Family Yuletide – *Early Dec - $15 adult, $5 children (ages 4-13) - check online for fees - reservations required.* At Christmastime, the stableyards at Middleton Place host a special night of wreath-making, storytelling around a fire, and other holiday happenings.

THE WILD SIDE OF MAGNOLIA PLANTATION

3550 Ashley River Rd., west of Drayton Hall - ☎843-571-1266 - www.magnoliaplantation.com - $15 adults, $10 children (ages 6-12) - Both the Zoo and Nature Center are open daily 8:30am-5pm. ♿*See p49.*

Nature Center – Little ones can pet animals like pygmy goats and white-tailed deer at **Magnolia Plantation★★**. There's even a food dispenser at the entrance, so they can feed the domestic animals.

Paolo's Italian Gelato

41 John St., Charleston. ☎843-577-0099. www.paolosgelato.com. What better way to end a visit to the Children's Museum than to go right across the street for a creamy gelato at Paolo's? This Italian version of ice cream is made fresh daily and comes in a bunch of yummy flavors—peach, chocolate, fig, strawberry basil, limoncello and many more—that the kid in everyone will love.

Nature Train – *Departs every half-hour from the depot near the main parking lot - $8 - children under age 6 free).* You never know what you might see aboard the train. Naturalists lead tours through the plantation's wetlands, and help you spot alligators, turtles, and marsh birds along the way.

Zoo – Children and their parents will both enjoy the zoo at where they will meet beavers, bobcats and birds of prey.

CHARLESTON MUSEUM FUN

360 Meeting St. - ☎843-722-2996 - www.charlestonmuseum.org. Kids of all ages will be excited by history at the **Charleston Museum★**. **Kids Tours** – Every Wednesday in June and July *(once a month the rest of the year)* at 3:30pm, these special guided tours (included with admission) focus on a particular artifact in the museum's collection, such as the Egyptian mummy or the dinosaur skeleton.

Kidstory – A hands-on exhibit Kidstory brings Lowcountry history to life for little ones.

Lowcountry Stories – Kids hear tall tales of the Lowcountry at this multimedia story-telling station.

JAMES ISLAND COUNTY PARK

871 Riverland Dr., on James Island - ☎843-795-7275 - www. ccprc.com - Open daily 8am-sunset (times vary seasonally) - $2 (free for children under age 2). Do the kids need some space to run? This 643-acre county park should do the trick. With picnic areas, ball fields, biking trails and creeks for fishing, there's plenty of recreation here. Rent a pedal boat, bicycle or kayak, or try scaling the 50-foot climbing wall.

151

Splash Zone

☎843-795-4386 - Open late May–mid-Aug daily 10am-6pm - Mid-Aug–Labor Day weekends only 10am-6pm - $9.99 adults, $8.99 children under 48-inches tall (free for children under age 2). Kids will go wild at the James Island's water park, which features a 200-foot tube slide, a 200-foot open slide, a 500-foot lazy river for tubing, and a Caribbean-themed water playground. And there's a regular pool, too (complete with lifeguards). Don't forget your swim suit!

Spas

Pounding the pavements in search of Charleston's fascinating history can be exhausting. Pamper those tired feet—and the rest of you—at some of the city's serene day spas.

THE DEWBERRY SPA

334 Meeting St., in The Dewberry hotel. ☏843-872-9094 - *www.thedewberrycharleston.com.*
Hidden away in a new luxury boutique hotel overlooking Marion Square, The Dewberry Spa fashions a cypress-lined sanctuary with hand-crafted wallpaper and fine art by Southern masters. A blend of antioxidants, sea extracts and botanicals—including the native dewberry plant—infuse

Earthling Day Spa

© Earthling Day Spa

treatments here with the essence of nature. Wrap yourself in a Carolina Cocoon of Lowcountry botanicals, herbs and rice, or indulge in a De-Stress package for two.

EARTHLING DAY SPA

245 E. Bay St. - ☏843-722-4737 - *www.earthlingdayspa.com.*
The former Roxy Theater, a block from the Old City Market, now houses this progressive spa, whose staff blends the Indian healing techniques of Ayurveda with more traditional services. Float away into Heavenly Bliss with the package of the same name. It combines an hour-long Sugar Glow Massage with a Ayurvedic Scalp Massage and finishes up with a facial.

LORDIS LOFT SALON & SPA

310 King St. - ☏843-789-3581 - *www.lordisloft.com.*
Conveniently located amid the blocks of retail on King Street, this Aveda day spa and salon is the place to recharge when you've had enough retail therapy. A full list of spa services ranges from mani-pedis to botanical skin resurfacing. A deep-tissue massage will soothe those tired muscles, and to really insure that you leave relaxed, you can add hot stones to any massage. While you're there, why not get your hair done too?

SPA ADAGIO

387 King St., in the Francis Marion Hotel - ☎843-577-2444 - www.spaadagio.com.

Renovated in early 2018 with a fresh, new look, Spa Adagio's services range from a hydrating coconut-oil massage to a restorative facial that incorporates stem-cell serum. Sugar scrubs and milk and honey wraps exfoliate and moisturize. And for men, the Gentlemen's Sport Facial is a 45-minute deep-cleansing treatment. When at last you're ready to leave this Historic District spa, you'll depart either with a spring in your step or slowly, in tempo adagio.

THE SPA AT BELMOND CHARLESTON PLACE

205 Meeting St., on the 4th floor of the Belmond Charleston Place hotel - ☎843-937-8522 - www.belmond.com/ charleston-place.

You'd expect the spa at this luxe Belmond property to be something special—and it is. The Euro-style retreat offers a full range of massage, body wraps, facials, pedicures and manicures in an atmosphere graced by imported Mexican floor tile and blond wood tones. Men are welcomed here with such treatments as the Facial and Feet First. At the adjacent health club, you'll find a range of fitness classes as well as a heated swimming pool, sauna and Jacuzzi. Stay for lunch and sample the spa menu—it may be low on fat, but it's high on taste.

STELLA NOVA

2048 San Rittenberg Blvd., West Ashley (second location in Mt. Pleasant) - ☎843-766-6233 - www.stella-nova.com.

Stop by this West Ashley retreat for an aromatherapy massage or a signature facial, or make a day of it and mix and match your treatments. You might go for the 30-minute Stellar Salt Scrub, a body exfoliation using Dead Sea salts and pure plant oils, or a 60-minute Lavender Fields Wrap that soothes and rehydrates your skin with essential lavender oil. For skin that's been overdone by the sun, the Natura Bisse Age-Defying Face employs amino acids, vitamins and isoflavones to send you off looking and feeling younger.

THE SANCTUARY SPA AT KIAWAH ISLAND RESORT

1 Sanctuary Beach Dr., Kiawah Island, SC, 21 miles south of Charleston - ☎843-768-6340 - www.kiawahresort.com.

It's worth the half-hour drive from Charleston out to Kiawah Island to sample the spa at The Sanctuary luxury resort hotel. This high-end spa feels like a gracious Southern porch with its potted plants, trickling waterfalls and chaise lounges. Natural light floods each of the 12 rooms, where such treatments as the Ocean Fossil Fusion (incorporating detoxifying minerals from the earth and sea) are inspired by the ocean, maritime forest and lush gardens that form the setting for the resort.

Golfing

Whether or not Charleston is, as it claims, the site of America's first golf course, is a matter of debate. What's not debatable is that the area sports some great courses. Including the world-famous resort courses at Kiawah Island and Wild Dunes, the Charleston area counts 20 golf courses open to the public. Kiawah and Wild Dunes resorts, as well as many Charleston hotels, offer golf packages. Ask about package rates when you make your reservation.

For a complete list of area links, check online at: www.charlestongolfguide.com.

CHARLESTON GOLF COURSES

Charleston National Country Club – *1360 National Dr., Mt. Pleasant -* ℘*843-884-4653 - www.charleston nationalgolf.com.* Hailed for its beauty, this challenging Rees Jones-designed course skirts marshland and natural lagoons.

City of Charleston Golf Course – *2110 Maybank Hwy. -* ℘*843-795-6517 - www.charleston-sc.gov/golf.* Opened in 1929, this public municipal course has six sets of tees to accommodate all skill levels.

Dunes West Golf Club – *3535 Wando Plantation Way, Mt. Pleasant -* ℘*843-856-9000 - www.golfdunes westgolfclub.com.* Sister course to Wild Dunes, the par-72 Dunes West is located on the site of historic Lexington Plantation.

The Links at Stono Ferry – *4812 Stono Links Dr., Hollywood -* ℘*843-763-1817 - stonoferrygolf.com.* The Battle of Stono Ferry was fought in 1779 on the grounds now occupied by this semi-private championship course.

Patriots Point Links – *1 Patriots Point Rd., Mt. Pleasant -* ℘*843-881-0042 - www.patriotspointlinks.com.* You get golf with a view of ocean-bound cargo ships here, since Charleston Harbor's shipping lanes lie just offshore.

Greens fees

In the Charleston area, greens fees can run as low as $40 for a city course to more than $250 for the resort courses, depending on the course, the season, the day of the week, and the time of day you play. Generally, greens fees are less expensive on weekdays and later in the afternoon. You'll often get the best deals in off-season, which in Charleston is from June to September and from December through January.

Gator on the Green

Don't panic if you spot an alligator on the green. These critters are a common sight on many Lowcountry courses, especially those that border marshland (such as Kiawah and Wild Dunes). If you leave the alligators alone, they'll usually let you play through—just don't try wrestling an alligator for your ball.

RESORT COURSES

You don't have to stay at Wild Dunes (♿see p. 90) or Kiawah Island (♿see p. 81) in order to play their top-notch greens, but if you're not staying at the resorts, you can't book tee times more than seven days in advance. Off-season rates apply from December through February in the resort areas.

Kiawah Island★★

Kiawah claims five public golf courses (the River Course is reserved for property owners), including the world-renowned Ocean Course, which hosted the PGA Championships in 2012, and will again in 2021.

Cougar Point Golf Course – *West Beach Village* - ☏*843-266-4020.* This course reopened in 2017 after an extensive renovation.

Oak Point Golf Course – *4255 Bohicket Rd., Johns Island* - ☏*843-266-4100.* Undulationg fairways at Oak Point lie just outside the gate of Kiawah resort.

The Ocean Course – *1000 Ocean Course Dr., on Vanderhorst Plantation* - ☏*843-266-4670.* These wind-blown Pete-Dye-designed links have hosted each of the PGA's major championship tournaments.

Osprey Point Golf Course – *Vanderhorst Plantation* - ☏*843-266-4640.* Tom Fazio laid out Osprey Point around saltwater marshes.

Turtle Point Golf Course – *East Beach Village* - ☏*843-266-4050.* Rolling sand dunes edge this Jack Nicklaus-designed course.

Wild Dunes★

The private resort on Isle of Palms offers 36 holes of championship golf. Both Wild Dunes courses were designed by Tom Fazio. For tee times at both Wild Dunes course, call ☏855-998-5351.

Harbor Course – *5881 Palmetto Dr.* This challenging par-70 course has four holes along the Intracoastal Waterway.

Links Course – *5757 Palm Blvd.* The last hole of the top-rated Links Course overlooks the Atlantic Ocean.

On the Water

Since Charleston is surrounded by water and the Lowcountry is laced with marshes and tidal creeks, there's no excuse not to get out on the water. Here are a few ways to enjoy it.

PADDLE A KAYAK

Coastal Expeditions – *514 Mill St., Mt. Pleasant - across the river from the Historic District at the Shem Creek Maritime Center - ☏843-884-7684 - coastalexpeditions.com.* Paddling a sea kayak through the area's saltmarsh creeks, you can experience the Lowcountry in a way that few people do. These 3-hour naturalist-led tours *($65 adults, $45 children ages 12 and under)* include basic instruction and are suited to the novice. If you're proficient, you can rent kayaks and go off on your own *($45/half day, $55 full day).* Either way, you're bound to see marsh birds and other denizens of

The Charleston Angler

1113 Market Center Blvd., Mt. Pleasant (other location in West Ashley) - ☏843-884-2095 - www.thecharletonangler.com. Area fly fishermen stop first at The Charleston Angler, which has everything from live bait to the best names in rods. The helpful staff, avid anglers themselves, will fill you in on recent fishing conditions and catches, and answer any questions you might have.

the tidal creeks, as well as the shrimp boats that dock at Shem Creek.
Charleston Outdoor Adventures
1871 Bowens Island Rd. - ☏843-795-0330 - www.charlestonoutdoor adventures.com. Professional guides lead 2- and 3-hour kayaking expeditions through the calm saltwater creeks behind Folly Beach. On the 2-hour tour *($47 adults, $27 children 12 and under)*, you'll paddle past wading birds and barrier islands—and, if you're lucky, you may even spot some dolphins.

SAIL AWAY

Schooner Pride – *Departs daily from Aquarium Wharf, 360 Concord St. - ☏843-722-1112 - www.schoonerpride. com - Call for schedules - $40 adults, $30 children (age 11 and under).* Hop aboard this 84-foot-long, 3-masted Class "C" tall ship for a look at Charleston the way the early settlers saw it—from the decks of their ships. Resembling a 19C trading schooner, the 49-passenger vessel glides silently on its two-hour cruise. If you're feeling adventurous, the crew might just let you help trim the sails or have a turn at the helm.

Ocean Sailing Academy – *20 Patriots Point Rd., Mt. Pleasant - ☏843-971-0700 - orasail.com.* Want to learn to sail? Join a small group of beginners and a certified instructor for a 3-hour Introduction to Sail course *($95/*

Edwin S. Taylor Folly Beach Fishing Pier

person) aboard an untippable 26-foot keelboat at this sailing academy located on Patriots Point. Call a week in advance to make a reservation (*daily 8am-6pm*).

GO FISH

Dropping your line off a pier doesn't require a fishing license, but more serious angling, both fresh- and saltwater, does. For fishing information and fees, check online at the **Marine Resources Division of the South Carolina Dept. of Natural Resources**: www.dnr.sc.gov. Depending on the time of year, you can catch redfish, sea trout, tarpon, Spanish mackerel and jack crevalle in area waters.

Fishing Charters
For offshore and inshore charters, contact the following operators:
Absolute Reel Screamer Charters – *Depart from 2223 Folly Rd -* ☎*843-270-4464 -* *www.follybeachcharters.com.*
Aqua Safaris, Inc. – *Charleston Harbor Marina at Patriots Point -* ☎*843-886-8133 - aqua-safaris.com.*

Fin Stalker Charters – *Depart from various points -* ☎*843-509-9972 -* *www.finstalker.net.*
The Reel Deal Charters, LLC – *Depart from various points -* ☎*843-388-5093 - www.thereeldealcharters.com.*
Reel Fish Finder Charters – *Depart from various points -* ☎*843-697-2081 - reelfishfinder.com.*

Fishing Piers
If you want to go it alone, try casting your line from one of the Charleston area's fishing piers:
Edwin S. Taylor Folly Beach Fishing Pier – *101 E. Arctic Ave., Folly Beach -* ☎*843-762-9516 - www.ccprc.com - Open daily 7am–sunset (hours vary seasonally) - $10 adult non-residents, $3 children.*
Waterfront Park Pier – *Cumberland St. to Tradd St. -* ☎*843-724-7321 - www.charlestonparksconservancy.org - Open daily sunrise–sunset.*
James Island County Park Dock – *871 Riverland Dr., on James Island -* ☎*843-406-6990 - www.ccprc.com - Open daily 8am–sunset (hours vary seasonally) - $2 park admission.*

Places to picnic

Surrounded by water and punctuated with lovely parks, Charleston's peninsula boasts a wealth of idyllic places to picnic.

FIND A PARK

When you need a break from sightseeing, enjoy lunch outdoors in one of these spots.

Waterfront Park★ – *On the Cooper River at the end of Vendue Range.* Spread a blanket on the grass or settle into one of the wooden swings on the pier and keep an eye out for dolphins.

White Point Gardens★ – *Along the Battery, at E. Bay St. and Murray Blvd.* Set at the tip of the peninsula, White Point boasts a rich history along with river views (🕘*see p. 37*).

Hampton Park – *30 Mary Murray Dr.* Stake out a picnic table at this landscaped 70-acre park, named for Civil War general Wade Hampton.

James Island County Park – *871 Riverland Dr., on James Island.* The county park is equipped with covered picnic shelters and grills (🕘*see p. 151*).

Marion Square – *Corner of King and Calhoun Sts.* Lay out a blanket on this 6.5-acre green space, a landmark in the center of the Historic District.

PACK A PICNIC

Stock your picnic basket with gourmet provisions from the fine purveyors below.

Bon Bahn Mi – *162 Spring St. - ℘843-414-7320 - bonbahnmi.com.* Pick your protein to sandwich inside a baguette along with cucumber, pickled carrots and daikon radish, cilantro, crispy shallots and chile mayo.

Butcher & Bee – *1085 Morrison Dr. - ℘843-619-0202 - butcherandbee. com.* Order up a mezze plate at this Mediterranean deli, and be sure to get a fresh-baked cookie for dessert.

Caviar and Bananas – *51 George St. - ℘843-577-7757 - www. caviarandbananas.com.* Duck confit with pickled red onions and fig preserves on sourdough will make any picnic special.

goat.sheep.cow. – *106 Church St. - ℘843-480-2526 - www. goatsheepcow.com.* Pick up a loaf of bread to pair with one of the custom cheese plates here.

Queen Street Grocery – *133 Queen St. - ℘843-723-4121 - queenstreetgrocerycafe.com.* Opened in 1922, this venerable grocery offers hot pressed sandwiches, plus salads and smoothies.

Ted's Butcherblock – *334 E. Bay St. - ℘843-577-0094 - www. tedsbutcherblock.com.* Meat is shaved to order for Ted's custom sandwiches and charcuterie plates.

Charleston specialties

From she-crab soup to shrimp and grits, the soul of Charleston and the Lowcountry lies in its cuisine. Named for the marshy prairies that line the low-lying South Carolina Coast north and south of Charleston, the Lowcountry boasts distinctive Southern-inflected food traditions that reflect a melting pot of different cultures from Europe, the Caribbean, and Africa.

A MELTING POT

As a city in South Carolina, Charleston takes its cuisine cues from classic Southern fare such as fluffy biscuits, fried chicken, cornbread, and field peas. From South Carolina come grits ground from local corn, and plentiful shrimp, crab and oysters—the trilogy of shellfish caught off the city's coast. Folks typically wash their meal down with a tall glass of **sweet tea**. If you order iced tea in Charleston, what you'll get—unless you specify otherwise—is this beverage brewed with plenty of sugar.

What makes Lowcountry cuisine unique are the flavors and ingredients that came from far away: rice, okra, and benne (sesame) seeds that the slaves brought with them from West Africa, and spices that came with settlers from the West Indies. With all these ingredients at hand, modern Charleston chefs are whipping up a sophisticated take on Southern fare.

No surprise that Charleston today is lauded for its stellar restaurants, serving everything from smoked brisket to shrimp and grits.

CREAM OF THE CROPS

Here are a few must-try dishes while you're in town. All these foods feature prominently on Charleston's restaurant menus and/or food shops.

Benne Wafers – Benne is the term African slaves used for sesame seeds, which they brought to the area from West Africa in the 17C. You'll find these wafers, in both sweet and savory versions, for sale in many shops in Charleston.

Carolina Gold Rice – This aromatic heirloom rice, which is thought to have been brought from Africa with the slaves, has been grown in the Lowcountry since the early 18C. Considered the grandfather of long-grain rice in the Americas, Carolina Gold is named for its golden hue in the fields.

Lowcountry Boil – A perfect dish for feeding a crowd, Lowcountry boil combines shrimp, sausage, corn, and potatoes, all cooked together in one big pot and piquantly seasoned.

Oyster Roast – If you're in town during the winter months, make it a point to experience this Lowcountry tradition. Oysters are properly roasted in a damp burlap bag placed on a metal plate over an open fire, and then piled, steaming, on tables for diners to shuck and eat, liberally doused with hot sauce.

Shrimp and Grits – Everyone seems to have his or her own version of this regional staple, an irresistible combination of local shrimp, fired up with spicy tasso ham and ladled over creamy stone-ground grits.

She-crab Soup – As the story goes, this cream-based soup was invented by a Charleston butler who added crab roe to the soup—thus the name—for a dinner in honor of President Taft. More often than not, it is served spiked with sherry.

Charleston Food Tours

One of the best ways to get an overview—and a taste—of Charleston's food heritage is to sign up for one of these delectable culinary walking tours.

Charleston Culinary Tours – *Departs from 5 Cumberland St., Mon-Sat 2pm (Thu and Fri 2pm and 3pm) - ☎843-259-2966 - charlestonculinarytours.com - $60/ person, reservations required.* This company's 2.5-hour Downtown Culinary Tour explores some favorite locally owned restaurants in the city's historic French Quarter.

Downtown's Local Flavors Tour

– *Departs from Broad and Church Sts. Mon, Tue, Fri and Sat 11am - ☎866-736-6343 - www.chow-downcharleston.com. $58/person.* This 3-hour epicurean tour will indulge your taste buds during six area stops.

Savor the Flavors – *Departs from 18 Anson St. daily 9:30am and 2pm - reservations required - ☎843-722-1100 - charlestonfootours.com - $60/ person.* Sip and sample some of the Lowcountry's most iconic foods— sweet tea, stone-ground grits, and benne wafers—during this 2.5-hour tour.

161

Charleston Recipes

No cocktail party in Charleston would be complete without a recipe from the pages of Charleston Receipts. The book, first published in November 1950, ranks as the oldest Junior League cookbook still in print. Originally conceived as a fundraising project for local charities, the 350-page cookbook contains 750 recipes (called "receipts" long ago), gathered from Charleston residents. The first edition of 2,000 copies sold out in four days. To date, more than 750,000 copies have been printed.

Charleston Receipts makes a great gift, or a souvenir of your trip—especially if you want to entertain like a local (see the section of recipes for traditional Southern punches). Pick up a copy at the Shops of Historic Charleston Foundation Shop (108 Meeting St.) or in bookstores and cooking shops around town.

Planning Your Trip

South Carolina palm trees
©NDJordan/Michelin

Know before you go

ENTRY REQUIREMENTS

Visitors from outside the US can obtain information from the Charleston Convention and Visitors Bureau *(www. charlestoncvb.com)* or from the US embassy or consulate in their country of residence. For a complete list of American consulates and embassies abroad, visit the US State Department Bureau of Consular Affairs listing on the Internet at *www.usembassy.gov.*
Identity papers – Travelers entering the US under the **Visa Waiver Program** (VWP) must have a machine-readable passport valid 6 months beyond their expected stay. Any traveler without a machine-readable passport will be required to obtain a visa before entering the US. Citizens of VWP countries are permitted to enter the US for general business or tourist purposes for a maximum of 90 days without needing a visa. Requirements for the Visa Waiver Program can be found at the **Department of State's Visa Services website** (travel.state. gov). All citizens of non-participating countries must have a visitor's visa. Upon entry, nonresident international visitors must present a valid passport and a round-trip transportation ticket. Canadian citizens must present a passport, Enhanced Driver's License or a Trusted Traveler Program enrollment card (like NEXUS, FAST/EXPRES and SENTRI).

US Customs – All articles brought into the US must be declared at the time of entry. Prohibited items include plant material; firearms (if not for sporting purposes); meat and poultry products. For detailed information, contact the US **Customs and Border Protection**, 1300 Pennsylvania Ave. NW, Washington, DC 20229 (*877-227-5511 or 202-325-8000 if calling from outside the US - www.cbp.gov*).
Driving in the US – Visitors bearing a valid driver's license issued by their country of residence are not required to obtain an International Driver's License. Drivers must carry vehicle registration and/or rental contract, and proof of automobile insurance at all times. Gasoline is sold by the gallon (1 gal=3.78 liters). Vehicles in the US are driven on the right-hand side of the road.
Time Zone – Charleston is located in the Eastern Time Zone (the same time zone as New York City), five hours behind Greenwich Mean Time.

GETTING TO CHARLESTON
BY TRAIN

Amtrak provides service to North Charleston (8mi north of downtown). The rail station is located at 4565 Gaynor Avenue in North Charleston. For rates, schedules and reservations, contact Amtrak: *800-872-7245* or www.amtrak.com.

BY PLANE

Charleston International Airport (CHS) is located 12 miles west of downtown off I-526 *(5500 International Blvd. -*

*843-767-7000 - www.chs-airport.com). Delta, American, United, Southwestern, Alaska and JetBlue airlines all have flights in and out of Charleston.
For information on getting to downtown from the airport, *see p 3.

BY BUS

For departures or arrivals by bus, the **Greyhound Terminal** is located in North Charleston (3610 Dorchester Rd. - 843-744-4247). For rates, schedules, reservations, contact **Greyhound**: *800-231-2222 - www.greyhound.com.

BY CAR

Charleston lies about 52 miles south-east of I-95, the main north-south corridor on the East Coast. From I-95, or approaching from farther west, take I-26 directly to the city.

MONEY AND CURRENCY EXCHANGE

Visitors can exchange currency downtown at **American Express Travel Service** at Abbot & Hill Travel (10 Carriage Lane - *843-556-9051). For cash transfers, **Western Union**

(*888-539-1108 - www.western union.com) has agents throughout the area. Banks, stores, restaurants and hotels accept travelers' checks with photo identification.

To report a lost or stolen credit card:
American Express (*800-528-4800)
Diners Club (*800-234-6377)
MasterCard (*800-627-8372)
Visa (*800-847-2911).

SEASONS

With its subtropical climate, the South Carolina Coast is a great place to visit year-round. The best times to come, weather-wise, are spring and fall, when high temperatures range in the mid-70s and Charleston is also the most crowded. **Spring**, when many festivals are held, is lovely in Charleston. **Summers** in the Lowcountry are hot (90s) and humid, but that doesn't stop sun-seekers from packing the beaches up and down the coast. In **fall**, the beach crowds go home, and golfers turn out in droves to enjoy the crisp, clear weather on area courses. **Winter** is usually mild—it's not uncommon to have 60-degree days in January, when hotel rates in Charleston plummet.

AVERAGE SEASONAL TEMPERATURES IN CHARLESTON				
	Jan	Apr	Jul	Oct
Avg. High	58°F/14°C	74°F/23°C	89°F/32°C	76°F/24°C
Avg. Low	40°F/4°C	57°F/14°C	73°F/23°C	60°F/16°C

IMPORTANT PHONE NUMBERS	
Emergency (24/7 - police, ambulance, fire)	☎911
Police *(non-emergency, Mon–Fri 9am–6pm)*	☎800-577-7434
Poison Control	☎800-222-1222
Medical Referrals Bon Secours-St.Francis/Roper Hospital East Cooper Regional Medical Center Medical University of South Carolina (MUSC) Trident Health System	☎843-402-1000 ☎843-881-0100 ☎843-792-2300 ☎843-797-7000
Dental Emergencies: MUSC College of Dental Medicine	☎843-792-2101
24-hour Pharmacy: Walgreens, 380 King St.	☎843-714-6243

ℹ INFORMATION

Contact the following organizations to obtain maps and information about sightseeing, accommodations, travel packages and seasonal events. Visitor centers below are closed Jan 1, Thanksgiving Day & Dec 25:

Visitor Centers

Charleston Visitor Center
375 Meeting St., Charleston - ☎800-774-0006 - *www.charlestoncvb.com. Open Apr–Oct daily 8:30am-5:30pm, Nov-Mar daily 8:30am-5pm.*

Kiawah Island Visitor Center
22 Beachwalker Dr., Kiawah Island - ☎800-774-0006 - *www. charlestoncvb.com - Open year-round Mon-Fri 9am-3pm.*

Mount Pleasant Visitor Center
99 Harry M. Hallman Jr., Blvd., Mt. Pleasant - ☎800-774-0006 - *www.charlestoncvb.com - Open year-round daily 9am-5pm.*

North Charleston Visitor Center
4975-B Centre Pointe Dr., North Charleston - ☎800-774-0006 - *www.charlestoncvb.com - Open year-round Mon-Sat 10am-5pm, Sun 1pm-5pm.*

Santee Welcome Center
Southbound I-95 at Santee - ☎803-854-2442 - *www.discover south carolina.com - Open year-round daily 9am-5pm.*

Helpful websites

Here are some additional websites to help you plan your trip:

www.charlestonlowcountry.com
www.discovercharleston.com
www.charlestonsfinest.com
www.charleston.com
www.nps.gov/nr/travel/charleston

Basic information

ACCESSIBILITY

Disabled Travelers – Federal law requires that businesses (including hotels and restaurants) provide access for the disabled, devices for the hearing impaired, and designated parking spaces. For further information, contact the **Society for Accessible Travel and Hospitality** (SATH), *347 Fifth Ave., Suite 605, New York, NY 10016 - ℘212-447-7284 - www.sath.org*). All national parks have facilities for the disabled, and offer free or discounted passes.

For details, contact the **National Park Service (Office of Public Inquiries**, *Department of the Interior, 1849 C St. NW - Room 1013, Washington, DC 20240 - ℘877-772-1213 or ℘800-325-0778/TTY - ww.nps.gov*). Passengers who will need assistance with train or bus travel should give advance notice to **Amtrak** (℘800-872-7245 or ℘800-523-6590/TDD - *www.amtrak.com*); or Greyhound (℘800-752-4841 or ℘800-345-3109/TDD - www.greyhound.com*). Reservations for hand-controlled rental cars should be made in advance with the rental company.

Local Sources – The following organizations provide detailed information about access for the disabled in Charleston:

♦ Access **www.charlestoncvb. com/visitors/travel_support/ accessibility.html** for information regarding accessibility. The visitor's bureau will mail you a printed copy if you are unable to access the guide online: ℘800-774-0006.

♦ Contact the **Charleston Area Regional Transit Authority** (CARTA) for information about disabled access to public transportation: ℘843-724-7420 - *www.ridecarta.com*).

♦ **S.C. Dept. of Disabilities and Special Needs**: ℘888-376-4636 - *www.ddsn.sc.gov*.

♦ **The Disabilities Board of Charleston County**: ℘843-805-5800 - *www.dsncc.com*.

ACCOMMODATIONS

167

For a list of suggested accommodations, ♿see p. 134.

Hotel Reservations
Historic Charleston Bed & Breakfast – ℘843-722-6606 or ℘800-743-3583 - *www.historic charlestonbedandbreakfast.com*.
Lowcountry Reservation Service – Located at three area visitor centers, this service offers in-person, same-day reservations for area hotels—often at a discount. This is a walk-in service only.

Hostels
A no-frills, inexpensive alternative to hotels, hostels appeal to budget travelers and students.
Not So Hostel – *156 Spring St. and 33 Cannon St. - ℘843-722-8383 - www.notsohostel.com - $28/night*

MAJOR HOTEL AND MOTEL CHAINS WITH LOCATIONS ON THE SOUTH CAROLINA COAST

Property	✆Telephone	website
Best Western	877-237-8791	www.bestwestern.com
Comfort & Clarion Inns	877-237-8791	www.choicehotels.com
Days Inn	800-225-3297	www.daysinn.com
Hampton Hill	800-445-8667	www.hamptoninn.com
Hilton	800-445-8667	www.hilton.com
Holiday Inn	888-465-4329	www.holidayinn.com
Sheraton/Starwood	800-325-3535	www.sheraton.com
Radisson	800-967-9033	www.radisson.com
Ramada	800-854-9517	www.ramada.com
Westin/Starwood	800-937-8461	www.westin.com

(dorms) - $68-$88/night (private rooms). Located in a residential area downtown, the Spring Street hostel comprises three mid-19C houses with air-conditioned rooms, shared baths and kitchen. The Cannon Street hostel lies five blocks away. Breakfast, Wifi and off-street parking are included.

BIKING

Biking is a popular pastime in The Holy City, which has been designated as a Bicycle-Friendly Community by the League of American Bicyclists. If you want to join the fun and forego the hassles and money involved in parking on the peninsula, Charleston's flat landscape makes biking a breeze. To get your bearings when biking around the peninsula, check out the **City of Charleston's interactive bike map** online: gis.charleston-sc.gov/interactive/bike.

Bike Rentals

Here are a couple of good places to rent bikes in Charleston:
Affordabike – 534 King St. This full-service bike shop offers a wide range of bicycles, from road to mountain versions, for both rent and purchase.

Holy Spokes Official Charleston Bike Share – 7 Radcliffe St. - ✆843-804-6992 - charlestonbikeshare.com. Bike sharing in Charleston is a breeze. $8/hr gives you 24/7 access to bikes at more than 25 corrals located around the city. To find and reserve a bike, use the mobile app at **app.**

socialbicycles.com. When you're ready to return your bike, just lock it at one of the bike racks within the system area.

DRIVING IN CHARLESTON

Charleston is not laid out in a neat grid, but at 5.2 square miles, the peninsula on which the Historic District is located isn't difficult to navigate. Meeting Street and East Bay Street are the main access points from the interstate highways. King Street, which is one-way going toward the Battery on the other side of Calhoun Street, is a main commercial thoroughfare. As you're driving, be cautious around the ever-present horse-drawn carriages that take visitors through the historic downtown.
Use of a **car seat belt** is required in South Carolina, and child safety seats are mandatory for children under 6 years of age and 80 pounds.

Parking

Metered street parking is available in Charleston, but it can be scarce, especially in high season and during business hours. Parking garages are a better option. You'll find them located at Aquarium Wharf and throughout the downtown area.

ELECTRICITY

Voltage in the US is 120 volts AC, 60 Hz. Foreign-made appliances may require AC adapters (available at specialty travel and electronics stores) and North American flat-blade plugs.

GUIDED TOURS

From horse-drawn carriages to ghostly encounters, Charleston offers tours of every stripe.

Carriage tours

A great way to visit Charleston is by clip-clopping around the Historic District in a horse- or mule-drawn carriage. Along the way, your driver will provide a witty—though not always historically accurate—narration of local history and lore.
Carriages line up along Market Street at Anson Street near the Old City Market. Tours generally last an hour Here are a few favorites:
Charleston Carriage Works – 20 Anson St. - ✆843-779-1279 - mycharlestoncarriage.com.

169

Old South Carriage Company – 14 Anson St. - ✆843-723-9712 - www.oldsouthcarriage.com.

Palmetto Carriage Tours – 8 Guignard St. - ✆843-853-6125 - www.palmettocarriage.com.

Boat Tours

Cruising the rivers around the Charleston peninsula is a great family excursion. Call for schedules (they vary seasonally) before you go.

Dolphin Discovery Sunset Cruises – Depart from Isle of Palms Marina *(end of 41st Ave.; reservations required)* - ✆843-886-5000 - nature-tours.com.

Sandlapper Water Tours – Depart from the Maritime Center, 10 Wharfside St., next to the South Carolina Aquarium - ✆843-849-8687 - www.sandlappertours.com.

SpiritLine – Narrated harbor tours depart from Aquarium Wharf (and Patriots Point) - 360 Concord St. - ☎843-722-2628 - spiritlinecruises.com.

Bus tours

Pineapple Tour Group – Bus tours depart from the Charleston Visitor Center at 375 Meeting St. - ☎877-553-1670 - pineappletourgroup.com – **Gullah Tour** – Departs from the bus shed at 43 John St., across from the Charleston Visitor Center - ☎843-763-7551 - gullahtours.com. This 2-hour introduction to Charleston's rich African-American heritage, includes the Gullah culture (&see p. 178).

Ghost tours

170 A city as old as Charleston is bound to have its share of ghosts. The 90-minute walking tours listed below require reservations. Due to the potentially frightening nature of the tours, children under age 7 are not permitted.

The Ghosts of Charleston – Depart from Buxton Books at Concord & Cumberland Sts. - ☎843-723-1670 - www.tourcharleston.com.

Pleasing Terrors Ghost Tour – Depart from Washington Square Park (*80 Broad St., behind City Hall*) - ☎843-568-0473 - oldcharlestontours.com.

Ghost and Dungeon Walking Tour – Depart from 418 Anson St. - ☎843-766-2080 - bulldogtours.com.

Walking tours

Architecural Walking Tours of Charleston – Depart from Meeting Street Inn, 173 Meeting St. - ☎843-893-2327 or ☎800-931-7761 - www.architecturalwalkingtoursof charleston.com.

Charleston Sole – Tours begin behind the Old Exchange Building on East Bay St. - ☎843-364-8272 - www.charlestonsole.com.

Charleston Strolls – Depart from Mills House Hotel, 115 Meeting St. - ☎843-722-8687 - www.charleston strolls.com.

The Original Charleston Walks – Depart from the ticket office at 45 South Market St. - ☎843-408-0010 - www.charlestonwalks.com.

Tour Charleston – Depart from Buxton Books, 2 Cumberland St. - ☎843-606-6025 - www.tourcharleston.com.

PRESS

Local newspapers
The Post and Courier (postandcourier.com) Is the leading daily newspaper in Charleston. The paper's arts and entertainment supplement, Charleston Scene, is published Thursdays. Other local papers include **The Chronicle** (*www. charlestonchronicle.net*), an African-American weekly; **Charleston City Paper**, published weekly (*www. charlestoncitypaper.com*); **Skirt**, a free monthly magazine geared to women (*www.skirt.com*).

Magazines
The monthly **Charleston Magazine** is found in many hotel rooms. It is also available for sale in bookstores and grocery stores.

PUBLIC TRANSPORTATION

Charleston Area Regional Transportation Authority

CARTA runs an extensive network of public buses and trolleys linking downtown with West Ashley and North Charleston (☎843-724-7420 - *www.ridecarta.com*). Bus stops are marked with signs. Fare is $2 for a one-way trip (*exact change required; transfers cost 50¢*). Children under age 6 ride free with a paying passenger. Purchase bus passes online (www.ridecarta.com), from CARTA's downtown office (36 John St.), CARTA bus drivers (daily passes only), and the Charleston Visitor Center (375 Meeting St.).

- ◆ All-day pass – $7
- ◆ 3-day pass – $14
- ◆ 10-ride pass – $16
- ◆ 40-ride pass –$56

DASH Trolleys – Antique-looking green trolleys of the hop-on hop-off Downtown Area Shuttle (DASH) operate three routes on the Charleston peninsula from CARTA bus stops (free of charge - ☎843-724-7420 - www. ridecarta.com). Call for schedules or pick up a trolley map at the Charleston Area Visitor Center and look for the green and yellow CARTA bus-stop signs around town.

SIGHTSEEING PASSES

Before your trip, consider purchasing one of the two attraction passes that offer discounts to multiple area museums and historic sites.

Charleston's Museum Mile – This pass gives visitors a choice of four diverse admission packages, with themes relating to different periods of Charleston history, African-American heritage, and Charleston architecture. Tickets may be purchased online at CharlestonMuseumMile.org or in-person at any Official Charleston Area Visitor Center (♿ *p.166*).

Charleston Heritage Passport – Offers discounts to nine historic, architectural and cultural sites: the Aiken-Rhett House, Heyward-Washington House, Joseph Manigault House, Nathaniel Russell House, Gibbes Museum of Art, Charleston Museum, Edmondston-Alston House, Middleton Place, and Drayton Hall. Passports are only available at the Charleston Visitor Center (375 Meeting St.), the North Charleston Visitor Center (4975-B Center Point Dr.) and Mt. Pleasant Visitor Center (99 Harry M. Hallman Jr. Blvd.). $52.95 for a **2-day passport** - $62.95 for a **3-day passport** - $72.95 for a **7-day passport** - ☎843-853-8000 - *www.charlestoncvb.com/heritage-federation/passport.*

Senior Citizens

Many hotels, attractions and restaurants offer discounts to visitors age 62 or older (proof of age may be required). AARP (American Association of Retired Persons) offers discounts to its members (*601 E St. NW, Washington, DC 20049 - ☎888-687-2277 - www.aarp.org*).

SPECTATOR SPORTS

Charleston has several minor-league sports teams, and offers a year-round calendar of sporting events:

• **RiverDogs** – Class A baseball at Joseph P. Riley Park - ✆843-577-3647 - www.riverdogs.com.

• **SC Stingrays** – AA League ECHL hockey at North Charleston Coliseum - ✆843-743-3000 - www.stingrayshockey.com.

• **Charleston Battery** – A League soccer at Blackbaud Stadium, Daniel Island - ✆843-971-4625 - www.charlestonbattery.com.

For more information, consult the website for the **Charleston Metro Sports Council**: www.sportscouncil.org.

TAXES AND TIPPING

Prices displayed in the US do not include the Charleston sales tax of 9%, which is not reimbursable (1% sales-tax discount is given to citizens age 85 and older); the hospitality tax of 2%; or the hotel tax of 13.5%.
It is customary to give a small gift of money—a tip—for services rendered, to waiters (15–20% of bill), porters ($1 per bag), hotel housekeeping staff (at least $3 per day) and cab drivers ($1).

TAXIS

In town the major cab companies are:
Yellow Cab – ✆843-577-6565 - $7 flat rate on the peninsula - other rates at www.yellowcabofcharleston.com.
Charleston Green Taxi – ✆843-819-0846 - see flat rates at www.charlestongreentaxi.com.
Charleston Black Cab Company – ✆843-216-2627 - rates by zone at www.charlestonblackcab company.com.
Charleston Cab Company – ✆843-566-5757 - $7 flat rate within the peninsula - other rates at www.charlestoncabcompany.com.

Pedicabs and Rickshaws

"Saving soles" is what Charleston Rickshaw (✆843-723-5685 - charlestonrickshaw.com) and Charleston Pedicab (✆843-577-7088 - pedicabcharleston.com) are all about. You'll see their open pedal-powered rickshaw-like contraptions all over the Historic District. If you're tired of trekking the city's streets, catch a ride on one of these unique vehicles. The carts can carry two to three people. They offer door-to-door service, and will even transport your wedding guests—or the bride and groom—to the church on time.

Getting Hitched

*Thinking about getting married? With its lovely historic homes, lush gardens and beautiful beaches, Charleston makes a storybook setting for a wedding. Get all the information you need, from hair stylists to party halls, in the **Charleston Area Wedding Guide**, available from the Charleston Area Convention and Visitors Bureau (www.charlestonweddingguide.com).*

Water taxis

☎843-330-2989 - www.
charlestonwatertaxi.com - $12 for an
all-day pass. Plying the river hourly
from four locations (Waterfront
Park, Maritime Center, Patriots Point
and Charleston Harbor Resort in Mt.
Pleasant), water taxis are a fun way to
get around when the weather is nice.

TELEPHONE

Area Codes

To call between different area codes,
dial 1 + area code + seven-digit
number. It's not necessary to use the
area code to make a local call.
The area code for Charleston, Kiawah,
Isle of Palms, Myrtle Beach and Hilton
Head is **843**.

For Savannah and the Golden Isles of
Georgia, the area code is **912**. Within
the US, if a phone number begins with
800, 866 or 877 (these are toll-free),
you must first dial a 1 before the
number.

Traveling the coast

MYRTLE BEACH

Stop for information and maps at one
of these visitor centers:
Airport Welcome Center – 1100
Jetport Rd. - ☎843-626-7444 -
www.visitmyrtlebeach.com.
**Myrtle Beach Area CVB and Myrtle
Beach Welcome Center** – 1200
N. Oak St. - ☎843-626-7444 -
www.visitmyrtlebeach.com.

Getting there

By Air – Myrtle Beach **International
Airport** (**MYR**) is located south
of 17th Avenue off Hwy. 15 (*1100
Jetport Rd. - ☎843-448-1580 - www.
flymyrtlebeach.com*) and is served by
major and discount airlines. Rental-
car companies have facilities at the
airport.

By Car – Myrtle Beach lies roughly
halfway between New York City and
Miami, Florida and an hour's drive
from I-95, I-20, I-26 and I-40.

Getting there without a car

Greyhound buses (*www.greyhound.
com - ☎800-231-2222*) run from
Charleston to Savannah, GA,
Beaufort, SC, and Brunswick, GA.

Getting Around

Driving in Myrtle Beach – The Grand
Strand's commercial strip, Business 17,
can be frustrating to navigate,
especially in summer when families
flock here and the road seems more
like a parking lot (Myrtle's most
crowded period is 4th of July week).
All of Myrtle's major arteries parallel
the Atlantic Ocean. **Ocean Boulevard**

MEASUREMENT EQUIVALENTS										
Degrees Fahrenheit	95º	86º	77º	68º	59º	50º	41º	32º	23º	14º
Degrees Fahrenheit	35º	30º	25º	20º	15º	10º	5º	0º	-5º	10º
1 inch = 2.5 centimeters	**1 foot = 30.48 centimeters**									
1 mile = 1.6 kilometers	**1 pound = 0.45 kilograms**									
1 quart = 0.9 liters	**1 gallon = 3.78 liters**									

(Rte. 73) runs right along the Atlantic, from Myrtle Beach State Park to 79th Avenue North. **Kings Highway**, (Business 17), is the next road to the west. This often-congested thoroughfare branches off US-17 in Murrells Inlet and reconnects with it north of 79th Avenue. **US-17 Bypass** is the route to take if you want to avoid the main thoroughfare.

Beach Regulations and Safety

In Myrtle Beach, glass containers and alcohol are not permitted on the beach, and it is illegal to drive on the beach or to set off fireworks. No animals are allowed on the beach or on Ocean Boulevard from 13th Avenue South to 21st Avenue North at any time of the year. On other beaches, dogs are allowed on the beach only before 9am and after 5pm from May to Labor Day. Dogs must be on a leash at all times in public. Pet owners are responsible for picking up after their pets.

Pay attention to beach safety flags posted on the beach: yellow means a lifeguard is on duty; blue means it's dangerous to swim; red signals no swimming allowed. If you encounter a riptide—a strong current that can sweep you out to sea—don't try to fight it. Immediately yell for help. In the meantime, stay relaxed and swim parallel to the shore until you are free from the current's pull Contact these organizations for maps and information.

Savannah Convention and Visitors Bureau – 101 E. Bay St., Historic District - ☎912-644-6400 or ☎877-728-2662 - www.visitsavannah.com.

Golden Isles Convention and Visitors Bureau – 1505 Richmond St, Brunswick, GA - ☎912-265-0620 or ☎800-933-2627 - www.goldenisles.com.

SAVANNAH

Getting there

By Air – Savannah/Hilton Head International Airport (**SAV**), located 10 miles north of downtown, off I-95 (*400 Airways Ave. - ☎912-964-0514 - www.savannah airport.com*).

Two major airports provide service to **Georgia's Golden Isles**: **Savannah/ Hilton Head International Airport,**

© Gwen Cannon/Michelin

175

Litchfield Beach

85mi north of Sea Island via I-95; and **Jacksonville International Airport** (**JAX**), 70 miles south of Sea Island off I-95 (*400 Yankee Clipper Dr., Jacksonville, FL - ℘904-741-4902 - www.flyjax.com*).
Brunswick Golden Isles Airport s served by Delta Connection. 295 Aviation Pkwy., Brunswick, GA - ℘912-265-2070 - www.flygcairports.com.

By Car – From the north or south, reach Savannah and the Golden Isles via I-95, the main north-south corridor along the East Coast. From the west, get to Savannah via I-16, which intersects with I-75 in Macon, Georgia. If you're headed to the Historic Downtown, stay on I-16; it takes you straight into town.

Getting there without a car

Amtrak (www.amtrak.com - ℘800-872-7245) provides service on its Silver Service Palmetto train from Charleston to Savannah as part of its New York-to-Miami route.

Greyhound buses (*www. greyhound.com - ℘800-231-2222*) run from Charleston to Savannah, GA, Beaufort, SC, and Brunswick, GA.

Helpful Websites

Here are some additional websites to make it easy to plan your trip:
www.savannahchamber.com
www.visittybee.com.
www.coastalgeorgiaexperience.com

Festivals and events

Here is a sampling of some of Charleston's most popular annual festivals. For more monthly events, visit **www.charlestoncvb.com/events**.

FESTIVAL FUN IN CHARLESTON

Lowcountry Oyster Festival *Boone Hall Plantation, Long Point Rd., off US-17 in Mt. Pleasant -* ☎843-853-8000 - *www.charleston restaurant association.com/lowcountry-oyster-festival.* Native Americans introduced settlers to roasted oysters in the 17C, and today the Lowcountry oyster roast is a time-honored tradition. The self-proclaimed "world's largest oyster festival" takes place each year in late January or early February. When they say "large," they're not kidding: 80,000 pounds of select oysters are trucked to the grounds of Boone Hall Plantation each year.

Southeastern Wildlife Exposition *Marion Square and other locations.* ☎843-723-1748 - *sewe.com.* You don't have to be a sportsman to enjoy this wildly popular festival, which celebrated its 34th year in February 2017. The largest event of its kind in the US, SEWE plays host to hundreds of artists and exhibitors, plus experts in wildlife and nature art. Conservationists, artists and animal lovers all find something to like in the three days of fun centered in Marion Square, including retriever

dog demonstrations, a wildlife sanctuary show, food demonstrations by local chefs, and an exhibit area encompassing fine art, sporting equipment and canine rescue groups.

Charleston Wine + Food Festival *Marion Square and various other venues.* ☎843-727-9998 - *charlestonwineandfood.com.* Take a heaping helping of accclaimed Charleston chefs, add a few handfuls of national vintners and mixologists, stir in top chefs from across the US, and you have a gourmet recipe for a good time. Held the first weekend of March each year, five days of foodie fantasy with more than 100 events begin on Wednesday night with the **Opening Night** party, devoted to local culinary talent. To taste the combined skills of Charleston chefs working with top chefs from across the US, make reservations for one of the **Signature Dinners** at area restaurants on Thursday, Friday and Saturday nights. During the day, watch cooking demonstrations, sample gourmet products, and taste a cluster of wines in the **Culinary Village.** There are also wine, beer and cocktail seminars, cookbook signings, luncheons and boat trips. Festivities wind up deliciously on Sunday with the **Harlem + Hominy Gospel Brunch** in the morning, and a barbecue bash called **Toasted** in the evening. Events sell out early, so don't wait to purchase tickets (on sale in September).

Festival of Houses and Gardens

Historic District - ☎843-722-3405 - www.historiccharleston.org. Here's your opportunity to peek inside some of the Historic District's loveliest private homes. Every spring (mid-Mar to mid-Apr), a host of residents open their doors to the public. During this month-long festival, which celebrated its 70th year in 2017, you can choose among tours that take in private homes in 11 different neighborhoods. Spring is one of Charleston's high seasons, so make reservations for this popular event well in advance.

Cooper River Bridge Run

☎843-856-1949 - bridgerun.com. Charleston's ever-popular 10K race, the Cooper River Bridge Run draws runners from around the US. Held in April, the run starts in Mt. Pleasant, crosses the Arthur Ravenel Jr. Bridge—which is closed to vehicles for the race—and ends in downtown Charleston. A **Kids Run** is held in Hampton Park the day before the race.

Spoleto★★

Various locations around the city - ☎843-722-2764 - spoletousa.org - (●see p. 130). Playing up international performing arts, this 17-day festival beginning in late May was founded in 1977 by Maestro Gian Carlo Menotti as the counterpart to his Festival of Two Worlds in Spoleto, Italy. Spoleto's little sister, **Piccolo Spoleto★** runs concurrently with the big event, and spotlights local and regional talent.

Patriots Point 4th of July Blast

Patriots Point, off US-17 in Mt. Pleasant - ☎843-884-2727 - www.patriotspoint.org. What could be more patriotic than fireworks launched from the deck of the World War II aircraft carrier USS *Yorktown*? Come see for yourself as Charleston celebrates the 4th of July at Patriots Point. Enjoy live bands, food, crafts, and the Kidz Zone play area starting at 4pm, and stay for the fireworks, which burst into the air just after 9pm.

Holiday Parade of Boats

☎843-724-7414 - www.charlestonparadeofboats.com. Stake out your place early (parade begins at 5pm) at one of the official viewing sites (Waterfront Park; along the Battery; and the USS *Yorktown* at Patriots Point) for this Charleston holiday tradition. Held each year in early December on Charleston Harbor, the parade features 50 vessels, decked out with lights and holiday finery, which make their way from Mt. Pleasant down the Cooper River, and along the Battery to the Ashley River. A fireworks finale lights up the sky above Castle Pinckney.

177

ANNUAL EVENTS

January

▶**Lowcountry Oyster Festival**:
A Lowcountry food tradition at Boone Hall Plantation, Mt. Pleasant, SC - www.charlestonrestaurantassociation.com (●see p. 176).

▶**Charleston Jazz Festival**:
Celebrate the Holy City's rich jazz
heritage and thriving jazz scene in
5 days of performances - various
venues in Charleston -
www.charlestonjazz.com/festival.

February

▶**Savanah Black Heritage Festival**:
Cultural, visual arts and performance
events - Savannah, GA - www.
savannahblackheritagefestival.com.
▶**Gullah Celebration**: Showcasing the
coast's Gullah culture at Hilton Head
Island, SC -
www.gullahcelebration.com.
▶**Southeastern Wildlife Exposition**:
A 3-day celebration of wildlife and
nature in downtown Charleston -
sewe.com (👆see p. 176).

March

▶**Charleston Fashion Week**:
Charleston's most fashionable
boutiques, emerging designers and
models strut their stuff in Marion
Square - charlestonfashionweek.com.
▶**Charleston Wine + Food Festival**:
In excess of 100 food- and wine-
related events - www. charleston
wineandfood.com (👆see p. 176).
▶**Festival of Houses and Gardens**:
(Mar-Apr) Tour some of Charleston's
Historic District homes - www.
historiccharleston.org/festival
(👆see p. 177).
▶**St. Patrick's Day Celebration**:
Green is the color and rowdy is
the mood in Savannah, GA - www.
savannahsaintpatricksday.com.

April

▶**Cooper River Bridge Run**: This
venerable race brings runners from
all over the state and beyond -
Charleston, SC - bridgerun.com
(👆see p. 177).
▶**Grand Strand Fishing Rodeo**: Two
days of wrangling for trophy fish -
Myrtle Beach, SC - www.facebook.
com/grandstrandfishingrodeo.
▶**Volvo Cars Open Tennis
Tournament**: Women's Tennis
Association pro tournament at
Family Circle Tennis Center on
Daniel Island (Charleston) -
www.volvocarsopen.com.

May

▶**Spoleto Festival USA**: (May-
Jun) Charleston's long-running
performing-arts festival - www.
spoletousa.org (👆see p. 130).
▶**Piccolo Spoleto**: (May-Jun)
Spotlights local artists and
performers - www.piccolospoleto.org
(👆see p. 130).
▶**World-Famous Blue Crab Festival**:
A weekend of local seafood and
beach music on the waterfront -
Little River, SC (Grand Strand) –
www.bluecrabfestival.org.

June

▶**Carolina Country Music Fest**:
The Southeast's premiere outdoor
country music festival, held on
the shores of Myrtle Beach, SC -
carolinacountrymusicfest.com.

July

▶**River Street 4th of July Celebration**: Rousakis Riverfront Plaza, Savannah, GA - www.riverstreetsavannah.com.

▶**Patriots Point 4th of July Blast**: Fun and fireworks by the Cooper River - Patriots Point, Mt. Pleasant, SC - www.patriotspoint.org (*see p. 177*).

September

▶**Charleston Water Sports Fest**: 7 days of competitive and recreational water sports - various locations in Charleston, SC - www.charlestonwatersportsfest.com.

▶**MOJA Arts Festival**: Charleston's 10-day celebration of Gullah culture - www.mojafestival.com.

▶**Savannah Jazz Festival**: A week of performances by international and regional jazz artists - Savannah, GA - www.savannahjazzfestival.org.

▶**Jekyll Shrimp and Grits Festival**: 3 days in mid-Sept - National Landmark Historic District, Jekyll Island, GA - www.goldenisles.com/events.

October

▶**Color of Music Festival**: For five days, black classical composers and musicians from around the world entertain in Charleston – www.colourofmusic.org.

▶**Beaufort Shrimp Festival**: A tasty celebration of SC wild-caught shrimp - Waterfront Park, Beaufort, SC - www.beaufortsc.org.

▶**Fall Tour of Homes & Gardens**: (month of Oct) Charleston's Historic District - www.preservationsociety.org.

▶**Latin American Festival**: Sights, sounds and tastes of Latin culture - Wannamaker County Park, North Charleston, SC - www.ccprc.com/1699.

▶**Oktoberfest**: German-inspired festivities include weiner dog races - River Street, Savannah, GA - www.riverstreetsavannah.com.

November

▶**Savannah Food & Wine Festival**: Highlights some of the South's best chefs, wine pros and beverage experts - Savannah, GA - www.savannahfoodandwinefest.com.

▶**Penn Center Heritage Days**: 3 days of Gullah history, folk arts, food and music - St. Helena Island, SC - www.penncenter.com/heritagedays.

▶**Holiday Festival of Lights**: (Nov-Jan) James Island County Park, Charleston, SC - www.ccprc.com.

December

▶**Holiday Parade of Boats**: Charleston Harbor, along the Cooper and Ashley rivers - www.charlestonarts.org (*see p. 177*).

▶**Holiday Tour of Homes**: Visit up to 8 private homes in the Historic District, Savannah, GA - www.savannah.com/events.

▶**Holiday Festival of Lights**: (mid-Nov-early Jan) Drive through the twinkling wonderland of lights at James Island County Park - www.holidayfestivaloflights.com.

Maps

Photo credits

Page 4
Charleston Historic District: © M. Linda Lee/Michelin
Drayton Hall: © Gwen Cannon/Michelin
Nathaniel Russell House: © M. Linda Lee/Michelin
Middleton Place and Gardens: © Middleton Place, Charleston, South Carolina
Fort Sumter National Monument: Courtesy of the National Park Service

Page 5
The Battery: © Walter Bibikow/age fotostock
South Carolina Aquarium: © South Carolina Aquarium
Patriots Point Naval & Maritime Museum: © Patriots Point Naval & Maritime Museum
Magnolia Plantation: Courtesy of the Charleston Area CVB, ExploreCharleston.com
Circular Congregational Church: © Doug Rogers/Michelin

- ◆ Charleston
- ◆ London
- ◆ New Orleans
- ◆ New York
- ◆ Paris

Visit your preferred bookseller for the short-stay series, plus Michelin's comprehensive range of Green Guides, maps, and famous red-cover Hotel and Restaurant guides.

THEGREENGUIDE short-stays **Charleston**

Editorial Director	Cynthia Ochterbeck
Editor	Sophie Friedman
Contributing Writers	M. Linda Lee
Production Manager	Natasha George
Cartography	Peter Wrenn, Nicolas Breton
Picture Editor	Yoshimi Kanazawa
Photo Researcher	Nicole D Jordan
Interior Design	Laurent Muller
Layout	Natasha George

Contact Us

Michelin Travel and Lifestyle North America
One Parkway South
Greenville, SC 29615
USA
travel.lifestyle@us.michelin.com

Michelin Travel Partner
Hannay House
39 Clarendon Road
Watford, Herts WD17 1JA
UK
℡01923 205240
travelpubsales@uk.michelin.com
www.viamichelin.co.uk

Special Sales

For information regarding bulk sales,
customized editions and premium sales,
please contact us at:
travel.lifestyle@us.michelin.com

Note to the reader Addresses, phone numbers, opening hours and prices published in this guide are accurate at the time of press. We welcome corrections and suggestions that may assist us in preparing the next edition. While every effort is made to ensure that all information printed in this guide is correct and up-to-date, Michelin Travel Partner accepts no liability for any direct, indirect or consequential losses howsoever caused so far as such can be excluded by law.

Tell us
what you think
about our products.

Give us your opinion:
satisfaction.michelin.com

MICHELIN

Michelin Travel Partner

Société par actions simplifiées au capital de 11 288 880 EUR
27 cours de l'Ile Seguin - 92100 Boulogne Billancourt (France)
R.C.S. Nanterre 433 677 721

© Michelin Travel Partner
ISBN 978-2-067230-20-0
Printed: April 2018
Printer: IME